The Mega System

Deciding. Learning. Connecting.

A Handbook for Continuous Improvement Within a Community of the School

Sam Redding

This handbook portrays the school as a system with many parts to be continuously engineered to precision by the community of people who have every reason to provide the best possible education for the children in their midst.

For more information about The Mega System, including downloadable forms and tools, see: www.adi.org/mega

Academic Development Institute
121 N. Kickapoo Street
Lincoln, IL 62656
217-732-6462
www.adi.org
Sam Redding: sredding@adi.org

ISBN: 0-9710077-1-3

This handbook is the product of the work of the LSS Mega Project staff at the Academic Development Institute and others at ADI who have devoted their thoughts and labors to helping schools improve so that each and every child may find avenues to success.

Research assistance by: Linda Searby and Pamela Sheley. Data analysis by: Janis Langdon and Joseph Meyer. Data management and editing assistance by: Rebecca Domkuski, Robin LaSota, Lori Thomas, and Luann Wooten. Input to school improvement processes by: Bernadette Anderson, Clare Eldredge, Karen Gerdts, Ron Hurley, Karen Huff-Cylc, Michael Koltun, Kathy Kurpeikis, Brenda May, Reatha Owen, Cheryl Patterson-Dreyer, Fred Plese, John Redding, and Barbara Thomas.

Publication Coordinator: Pamela Sheley
Graphic Designer: Sharon Newton

This research was supported in part by the Institute of Education Sciences (IES) of the U.S. Department of Education (ED) through its contract with the Mid-Atlantic Regional Educational Laboratory, the Laboratory for Student Success (LSS). The research was also supported in part by the Office of Innovation and Improvement (OII) of the U.S. Department of Education (ED) through a grant to the Academic Development Institute. The opinions expressed do not necessarily reflect the position of the supporting agencies, and no official endorsement should be inferred.

Acknowledgements

This handbook is offered
with acknowledgement of
the support, work, and example

of

James S. Coleman,
Herbert J. Walberg,
and Margaret C. Wang.

WHAT IS A MEGA SYSTEM?

What is a Mega System?

The term "mega system" derives from a field research project at the Laboratory for Student Success at Temple University that studied comprehensive school reform. Comprehensive school reform moves a whole school forward by dramatically changing the way it operates. This is a big (mega) picture approach to school improvement, requiring coherence among many component parts, in the way a system is a functioning whole with coherence among its parts. Comprehensive school reform attempts change in a school by first showing a model of the intended result and then carefully building toward that model by assembling the various parts. Sometimes this works, but often the model doesn't quite fit the particular school, critical parts are not constructed according to the plan, or the model, when properly assembled, fails to fly.

While still looking at the big picture, this handbook portrays the school as a system with many parts to be continuously engineered to precision rather than a static model to be replicated. The Mega System focuses on the internal operations of a school and the community of people who have every reason to provide the best possible education for the children in their midst. The incentive for improvement lies in parents' desire for their children to succeed and in the commitment to service of school people professionally equipped and empowered to pursue excellence in the community to which they belong. Devotion to children they know, love, and call by name is powerful motivation to constantly seek better ways to insure that each child meets standards of learning and is able to reach beyond those standards.

The Mega System abandons the replication of a prototype in order to chase the lodestar of student success; it swaps allegiance to program implementation for the corrective powers of timely data and sound research. The big picture is important, but so are the details. The indicators of a strong system of continuous improvement provided in this handbook enable the school, through its teams, to monitor its parts and subsystems, to test them against student learning outcomes. With experience, the teams modify and add to these indicators as they find their own avenues to success. The teams fine-tune the subsystems so that the school itself, the mega system, performs ever more effectively.

What Isn't Here?

Schools come in all shapes and sizes. Primary centers. Elementary schools. Middle schools. Junior high schools. High schools. Alternative schools. Public schools. Private schools. Parochial schools. Big schools and small schools. City schools and country schools. The Mega System described in this handbook strikes at the core of schooling, the hub that schools have in common— teaching and learning. The Mega System centers on the principal, teachers, students, and parents. This handbook describes the subsystems that are essential to effective schooling and how these subsystems function toward their own ends and also contribute to the chief purposes of the school as a whole.

Because this handbook focuses on systems rather than models, any school choosing to adopt its principles will make adjustments to fit its particular configuration. Even when a school gets the subsystems of the Mega System spinning efficiently, humming along with effective synchronicity, it will realize that other subsystems not described in this handbook must be organized and made to contribute to the overall purposes of the school. The Mega System does not outline systemic processes for extracurricular activities, guidance and counseling, after-school and tutoring programs, cafeteria operations, school maintenance, or transportation of students, yet these are all important functions in most schools. The Mega System's parsing of curriculum and instruction is most relevant to the core academic subjects, but its ideal of a standards-based curriculum delivered through highly individualized instruction is applicable with adaptations to special education, vocational education, the arts, and physical education.

While every subsystem is important to school improvement, the central components of deciding, learning, and connecting are paramount. The Mega System provides a solid point of departure, a way to put a school community on the track of continuous improvement. The Mega System provides basic training in school improvement. A good school will learn from it, adapt it, and reach well beyond it.

Table of Contents

Models, Systems, Communities

How do we best set schools on a course of continuous improvement? Thirty years of research supplies a consistent picture of what the most effective schools look like, but moving a particular school toward the ideal remains a thorny undertaking. Research also abounds with evidence-based practices, but the most scientifically credible of that evidence confirms very small and specific niches of teaching and learning. School personnel are not well equipped, nor do they have much time, to sort through the specifics, clump enough of them together to provide general direction, and apply the right practices to the school's unique situation. School reform models are an attempt to efficiently and coherently clump together an array of evidence-based practices to provide a picture with considerable detail. Yet, school reform models have struggled to demonstrate their ability to achieve significant gains in learning across a variety of settings and to internalize and perpetuate the processes that would continue to yield results.

RECOMMENDATIONS

a) Replace the static model with a system of continuous improvement.

b) Abandon the replication of a prototype and chase the lodestar of student success.

c) Swap allegiance to implementation for the corrective powers of timely data and sound research.

From 2000 to 2005, the LSS Mega Project was a field research project of Temple University's Laboratory for Student Success, one of the ten regional education laboratories supported by the U. S. Department of Education's Institute of Education Sciences. The Mega Project was launched in 2000 to study the burgeoning comprehensive school reform movement, with particular attention to Temple's own reform model, Community for Learning (CFL), which was adopted by more than 100 schools in the short span of three years when federal funding for comprehensive school reform became available in 1997. The LSS Mega Project staff has looked at school improvement from the inside, working closely with one reform model, school by school, and from the outside, studying implementation progress across the 100 schools. The project also followed the research literature that has tracked comprehensive school reform from its birth in the designs that emerged in the early 1990s to the implementation of those models in several thousand schools over the past several years.

This handbook is a mixture of research on school improvement and the Mega Project's practical experience with comprehensive school reform. The Mega Project's close look at school reform prompted a stream of questions for which project staff turned to the research literature and its own empirical examination for answers. These answers led to the chief recommendations herein: a) Replace the static model with a system of continuous improvement; b) abandon the replication of a prototype and chase the lodestar of student success; and c) swap allegiance to implementation for the corrective powers of timely data and sound research. These recommendations arise, in part, from frustration with comprehensive school reform (CSR). In so many schools, CSR came, ruffled feathers, and was gone, with little lasting consequence. But why? The models were sound, research-based, and proven in some contexts. They also were not based on esoteric methodologies or pedagogical rocket science, but on disciplined application of good practices that are on display in thousands of high-functioning schools every day.

Geoffrey Borman (2005) casts comprehensive school reform in a more positive light, demonstrating that the effect of CSR on student learning has been greater than the effect of Title I. Borman also shows that the most impressive gains in CSR schools come not during the three years of funded implementation, but in the fifth and subsequent years, with effect sizes accelerating in the out years. Despite these rosier views of the effects of CSR, Borman concedes that the effects of CSR are extremely variable. The characteristics of the model matter far less than the fidelity of implementation. According to Borman, "school-specific and model-specific differences in the ways that the components are actually implemented explain considerably more than simply knowing whether or not the CSR developer requires them" (p. 13). The success of school reform is tied most strongly to the level and quality of implementation. This caveat is the Achilles heel of model-based school reform. Implementation of a "model" has proven problematic. Knowing what a model school looks like is a different proposition from internalizing the processes of change and providing the incentives for success that result in continuous improvement.

High-functioning schools and schools cited for their "effectiveness" do the right things, do them well continuously, and always look for ways to improve. Dramatically changing the way a school operates when the school is not functioning well, as comprehensive school reform has attempted to do, takes time beyond the ordinary, an infusion of *new* time into a time-scarce system. Why is time so scarce in a system that has huge gaps of "downtime," most notably the summer months and ample holiday breaks? Teacher contracts bind them to duty for very few days and hours beyond the time students are present. Time for teachers to receive training or to meet and plan is confined to occasional, isolated, institute days and tiny slices of time before or after school. To carve deeper into teachers' contractual time is to take them away from students, and that seems counterproductive.

Schools that fail with comprehensive school reform do so not for lack of resources, other than time, but for want of determination and internal discipline. One is tempted to say to a school desiring improvement, "Here is a handbook. It will show you what has worked elsewhere, what research supports, and it will give you practical steps toward self-improvement. If you want it, make it yours." In essence, that is the purpose of this handbook: To place in the hands of school personnel who possess the determination and discipline for sustained improvement a coherent set of practices, a system if you will, that will serve them well. If they make it theirs. If they make it theirs, they will also find new time to get the job done.

Scheduling time to meet, train, and plan is a concrete objective. The school inclined toward improvement either finds the time or it doesn't. Will power and discipline sound like personality characteristics, and personalities are not easy to change. But in fact,

PURPOSE

In essence, the purpose of this handbook is to place in the hands of school personnel who possess the determination and discipline for sustained improvement a coherent set of practices, a system if you will, that will serve them well. If they make it theirs. If they make it theirs, they will also find new time to get the job done.

the strength of persistence (will power) and diligent execution of coordinated work (internal discipline) within an organization result in large part from the rewards and sanctions provided by the system as well as the opportunities for shared leadership toward clear goals. Getting these things right—rewards, sanctions, goals, and shared leadership—are, of course, part of continuous school improvement. They are, in fact, the foundation upon which it must be built. Because school is a supremely human enterprise, the relationships among its constituents are the connecting tissue of its system for improvement.

The determination and internal discipline to succeed, time to meet and plan, and a friendly handbook for guidance—those may be the ingredients of success. We fully understand, however, that something else may be required—a reason to seriously tackle school improvement and to stick with it. What is the incentive? What would motivate the people connected with a school to initiate a demanding system of improvement and persist with it? No Child Left Behind (NCLB) has made educators, and to some extent the public at large, cognizant that public schools should be accountable to the public for their performance. That performance is measured by the school's ability to move students, including disaggregated groups of students, to mastery of state learning standards and to provide a safe and orderly environment. NCLB's sanctions are viewed as punitive, for the most part, and applied only to "failing" schools. In fact, NCLB also encourages states to reward districts and schools for improvement in performance, and the philosophy of "no child" is that a single child should not be allowed to languish even within a school whose overall performance is exemplary.

While NCLB has provided a measuring stick for schools, a compelling incentive to engage in rigorous and continuous improvement must be found elsewhere. Who cares most about the school success of an individual child? Most assuredly, the child's parents do. NCLB attempts rather feebly to tap into the potentially powerful motivating factor of parents' concern for their own children with its choice option for schools that are failing. The effects of this limited parental choice have not been great, however, because: 1) the parents of a child who is not doing well but is attending a school that is meeting the minimum standard for progress do not have the option to switch schools; 2) choices available to many parents are limited, either because of geographic distance to a better school or because nearby schools are little better than the one the child would leave behind; and 3) the choice is limited to public schools.

How, then, might we tap parents' desire for their children to receive a good education as a motivating power in school improvement? How, in fact, might the strong professional desire of individual administrators and teachers to improve their schools and to advance the life opportunities for each and every one of their students propel continuous school improvement? The answer to both these questions lies in a system that candidly scrutinizes all its varied parts, holds them to the candle of sound research, examines their impact on each student's learning, and makes courageous decisions to get better. But a system of improvement is only part of the solution. The people who populate the system—students, parents, teachers, staff, volunteers—must share responsibility for the results, and they must understand clearly what is expected of them and how they can contribute. Beyond that, the system must include ways to reward success, in collective celebration and in recognition of individual excellence.

School reform *models* control the multitude of variables at play in a school by reducing the range of possible ways of doing things to a coherent core. Reform models are management templates, simplifying what is otherwise immeasurably complicated. The beauty of a school reform model is that it can establish coherence and order within a school. One problem with models is that they tend to be static, and their inflexibility can be frustratingly restrictive, creating a backlash of disillusionment, resentment, and resistance from school personnel. Another problem is that models are like glass attempting to cut a diamond; after much contact, the model is reshaped more than the school and loses its potency in the process.

A *system* is a group of linked parts that work together toward a common end. The commonly used term "school system" applies to a group of schools, organized into a district, and each school is a part in the system. But each school itself also operates as a system, with its own parts and subsystems, working toward its own ends. In the system of a single school, the state and the district serve as gatekeepers, regulating inputs to the system and monitoring its output—the learning its students acquire. The parts of the school's system include its internal decision-making structures, its policies and practices, its goals, its personnel and their various roles, its facilities, materials, and tools. The health and productivity of a system depend upon the quality of each of its parts and the effectiveness of their relationships to one another. Determining and improving quality requires methods for measuring the functioning of each part, each subsystem, and the system as a whole.

DEFINITIONS

School reform *models* control the multitude of variables at play in a school by reducing the range of possible ways of doing things to a coherent core.

A *system* is a group of linked parts that work together toward a common end.

DEFINITIONS

A **community** is a system of people, linked by their association with one another, their communication with one another, their allegiance to common values and purposes, and their assumed responsibilities and obligations to one another.

A **school community** consists of the people intimately attached to that school—teachers, students, parents of students, administrators, support staff, and volunteers.

A *community* is a system of people, linked by their association with one another, their communication with one another, their allegiance to common values and purposes, and their assumed responsibilities and obligations to one another. A *school community* consists of the people intimately attached to that school—teachers, students, parents of students, administrators, support staff, and volunteers. Community is the counterbalance to the cold, bureaucratic tendencies of public education, the formalities of organization that obscure the essentially personal and social purposes of schooling (Sergiovanni, 1999). The health and productivity of a school community depend upon the capacity of its members (human capital) and the quality of their relationships with one another (social capital).

A school is both an organized system and a community of people. It is a human enterprise. The expertise, motivations, rewards, and opportunities for association and communication of these people are essential to its effectiveness. The Mega System outlined in this handbook is an attempt to overcome the shortcomings of static models by internalizing systems for self-management that are guided by data and research. The Mega System is attentive to the human aspects of a school community whose purpose is to add significant value to the learning and life success of each of its students. The incentive to improve lies in parents' desire for their children to succeed, and in the commitment to service of school people professionally equipped and empowered to pursue excellence in the community to which they belong. Devotion to children they know, love, and call by name is a powerful motivation to constantly seek better ways to insure that each child meets standards of learning and is able to reach beyond those standards.

School Reform:
A Little Background

In the particulars of year-to-year life in an American school, teachers and principals try to navigate a course that is steady, comprehendible, and compatible with the context of their work. Stiff-arming each innovation that invades their province, they protect the integral core of professional endeavor, as they see it. This image presents competing forces—the inertia of everyday practice in schools and the erratic, short-lived, but momentarily vigorous assaults from the broader educational and political establishments. The erroneous conclusion may be drawn that these forces offset one another, and change is thwarted. In fact, they tend to moderate the excesses of one another, and change, viewed from a longer perspective, proceeds in a general course with constant self-correction.

Whatever the status quo in schooling, an alternative view will challenge it. Thus, we have competing visions of what schooling should be, and each vision might trace its philosophical ancestry through generations of previous visions, each contending for favor in its time. The starting point in this battle over how children are best educated might be placed within the lyceum of ancient Greece, in the Romantic challenge to Classicism (Hirsch, 2001), with the flowering of the American common school, at the rise of Progressivism (Chall, 2000; Ravitch, 2000), or anywhere else along the historical continuum. In every era, there is a status quo in schooling, and there is a challenge to it.

For sake of brevity, we will place our beginning point in 1983, with the publication of *A Nation At Risk: The Imperative for Education Reform*, by the newly-formed National Commission on Excellence in Education. The report boldly asserted that our nation was at risk because our public schools were failing to educate citizens capable of competing in a world economy that increasingly required a highly skilled workforce. As a consequence, the quality of individual life in the United States was diminishing, and the strength of the nation was declining. With this alarm call came a suggested direction, and that direction defines the integral core of professional endeavor to this day, and the assumed trajectory for what is to come.

Effective Schools

A Nation at Risk emerged from a backdrop of evidence about the possibilities for improved learning and the factors that contribute to it. The very idea that children's learning is significantly dependent upon the ways a school operated was asserted in the effective schools research in the 1970s (Edmonds, 1979). This paved the way for a national appeal for improvement of public schools in *A Nation at Risk*. The effective schools movement was itself a response to the 1966 Coleman Report (Coleman et al., 1966) that found scarce evidence of a relationship between a school's resources and its students' learning. While the Coleman Report emphasized the powerful influences of family background on children's learning, its principal author, James S. Coleman, refined this view in later writings (Coleman, 1981) and in comparisons between public schools and Catholic schools (Coleman & Hoffer, 1987). While adhering to his earlier finding that the level of resources in a school bore little connection to learning outcomes, Coleman did find that Catholic schools stressed academic rigor, order, discipline, time on task, and firm standards, and that these factors were predictive of greater learning. The same factors, he concluded, were also predictive of greater learning when found in public schools. Further, Coleman attributed the success of Catholic schools to the expectations they placed on parents, and the values and sense of community they nurtured among their staff, students, and families of students. Successful schools were able to restore the "social capital" that was being drained away from children by a society that increasingly separated adults, especially parents, from time with and connection to children (Coleman, 1987). These conclusions were very much in concert with the effective schools research which identified correlates of effective schools, including high expectations, frequent monitoring (measuring) of student progress, time on task, orderly environment, and home-school relations.

Standards and Assessments

The remedy for failing schools, as proffered by *A Nation At Risk*, was to transform the United States into a Learning Society, engaging every institution in life-long learning, delivered with excellence. The hallmark of this revolution would be "high standards," rather than minimum requirements. By elevating standards and expectations, levels of learning would rise, and our nation would be removed from risk.

School Reform: A Little Background

More than two decades after the publication of *A Nation At Risk*, we remain within the broad sweep of change toward schooling by standards. Over the course of those years, a thousand minor winds of innovation have blown, but the call to standards has weathered the storms and taken hold. The states have now adopted learning standards for children in their public schools. Student progress is measured with the yardstick of standards, and the process of measuring (assessment) has proceeded hand-in-hand with the establishment of standards. The measures are the standards-based assessments that states have instituted alongside the standards. Standards and measures are the legacy of *A Nation At Risk*, and they form the consistent and inexorable nucleus of change in public education.

TQM and Data-Based Decision-Making

In the 1980s, American business was highly influenced by Total Quality Management (TQM; Deming, 1986), which married three central principles regarding the success of an organization: 1) success is based upon the quality of the product or service as determined by its ability to satisfy the needs of the customer or client, 2) achieving quality comes from careful measurement of all systems and processes so that decisions are made from real-world data, and 3) quality is not a static condition, but a systemic devotion to continuous improvement. Thus, attention to the continuous improvement of systems, focus on outcomes, and data-based decision-making leaked into the school reform movement and found there a comfortable compatibility with standards and assessments. The Malcolm Baldrige model and the Malcolm Baldrige National Quality Award (given for organizations, including schools, that demonstrate quality principles) continue to apply TQM to the operation of schools.

Best Practices and Comprehensive Models

Along with the steady march of standards and measures came the search for methods that would boost children's learning so that they could meet the standards. Which practices were best? In what ways should schools reform themselves so that their students would measure up? What models of school practice could be held up as examples of success? These questions led to the cataloging of best practices, all supposedly validated by sound research, and the collection of practices into models for school improvement. The New American Schools Development Corporation was formed in 1991 (name changed to New American Schools in 1995) as a nonprofit corporation in conjunction with the America 2000 initiative of the first Bush administration. The purpose of New American Schools was to fund the development and dissemination of whole-school reform models. Models were accepted for funding based on competitive proposals, and the funding supported phases of development, implementation, demonstration, and scale-up. RAND Corporation was commissioned to provide evaluation of the project and a running account of the experiences of the models and the schools that adopted them. In 1997, Congress passed legislation to provide funding for schools that adopted models, thus accelerating the expansion of the models developed under New American Schools and bringing new models onto the scene. The legislation was rolled out by the U. S. Department of Education as the Comprehensive School Reform Demonstration Program (CSRD), and by 2002 whole-school designs had been adopted by more than 4,000 schools with Department of Education support (Berends, Bodilly, & Kirby, 2002).

Scientifically Based Research

With standards to measure against, state assessments to provide the measures, and competing reform models applying research-based best practices, the zeitgeist let loose by *A Nation at Risk* was sweeping forward as the twentieth century gave way to the twenty-first. Then the questions were raised: How *scientific* is the research underlying the best practices, and how rigorous is the evaluation applied to the reform efforts? The quantification of education was intensified in No Child Left Behind, the reauthorization of the Elementary and Secondary Education Act in 2001. At the same time, the U.S. Department of Education was reorganized around the premise that education must base its practices on scientifically based research, similar to the medical model. Impetus for this new focus on more rigorous research came from a variety of directions, including a report by a committee of the National Research Council (Shavelson & Towne, 2002). This report suggested ways the U. S. Department of Education could promote evidence-based policies and practices, placing education research within the scientific community with its own methods for rigorous research.

School Reform: A Little Background

Incentives

The chief alternative to whole-school reform is to provide rewards for success and let the school-based educators work out the details. Merit pay for teachers is an incentive system directed at the accomplishments of individual teachers. Other incentive systems reward the school for value-added performance. The underlying premise to an incentives-based approach is that there is no one best way to achieve educational excellence, and each school must be freed to pursue its own course, with incentives to encourage good results. School-level experimentation and accountability take preference over the adoption of external recipes (models or practices). The incentives might be provided for individual teachers, school leaders, or whole schools. The incentives would include monetary rewards and freedom from regulation. In the case of charter schools, freedom from regulation is often the incentive to propel studied experimentation, and the commitment of a school community charting its own destiny is the driving force. Within regular systems of public schooling, some states (Kentucky notably among them) have established formulas to channel increased funds to schools whose students demonstrate success in meeting standards (as evidenced on the state's assessments) and to provide oversight to those that lag.

The underlying premise to an incentives-based approach is that there is no one best way to achieve educational excellence, and each school must be freed to pursue its own course, with incentives to encourage good results.

Most incentives approaches are not contrary to the reigning regime of standards and assessments, but are a challenge to the whole-school reform movement. Given a climate of standards, assessments, and scientifically based research, schools (and their personnel), with proper incentives, will take self-correcting steps to improve their performance, and parents, given access to measures of school performance, will choose schools that get the results they desire for their children. Incentives are typically proposed by advocates of productivity; a careful analysis of the cost effectiveness of competing educational practices encourages decision-makers to weigh likely results in allocating resources and energies. Erik Hanushek (1994) asserts this point:

> We are persuaded that widespread use of appropriately designed performance incentives will bring positive results without large budget increases. Ample evidence can be found throughout industry and society to demonstrate that individuals respond to well-structured incentives. In a wide variety of circumstances, organizational objectives are better met through performance incentives than through regulations and administrative directives. (p. 5)

School choice is a challenge to both whole-school reform and external quantification of learning, and free market economics is the philosophical front-edge of the school choice movement. While a system of school choice may be positioned within structures of standards and assessments to guide parents' decisions, in the end, the consumer is supreme. Perhaps parents will choose schools that demonstrate success on standards-based assessments, and maybe these will be schools that have adopted particular school improvement models, but the incentive (typically a voucher) follows the choice of the child's parents and not the wishes of the state.

Cross Currents

Set a high bar for learning and calculate the percentage of students who clear it. If method X achieves a higher percentage of successes than method Y, then add X to the list of components in a system of education to be encouraged in schools, or let each school find its own mix of successful methods. Keep measuring and refining the methods until all children clear the bar, and then raise the bar. Reward schools that get the results, or at least give them a reprieve from punishment. This is the essence of school improvement at this juncture in history. But a consistent opposition has been voiced to what is perceived as the narrowing rigidity of standards and assessments and the efficacy of whole-school reform.

David Berliner and Bruce Biddle (1995) debunk what they call a manufactured crisis in education, claiming that *A Nation At Risk* was based on a false premise of the inadequacy of American schools. They revive the claim that the problem in American education is inequality of resource allocation rather than paucity of credible practice.

Robert Evans (1996) questions the sticking power of school change that is externally imposed, adopted under coercion, or accompanied by false promises and unrealistic expectations. Real and lasting change requires the internalized commitment of participants, not their grudging, minimal acceptance. The engines of change are personal and internal to the organization; they are imbedded in experience and able to overcome inertia and rise above predicted trajectories of results. "In the best of schools, with the best resources and the most skillful leadership, the time frame for transforming culture, structure, belief, and practice is years. Success will require the highest strivings

School Reform: A Little Background

and the most down-to-earth expectations. Only if we maintain a healthy respect for the lessons of experience can real hope truly triumph" (p. 299).

John Goodlad lambasts the school reform movement and the excesses to which standards and assessments have been applied, writing that

> Arguments for children's well-being, no matter how well grounded, rarely win the day in eras of school reform. The current testing crusade has now become politically correct. Counterarguments commonly receive the "you're against change" response. The data on the low correlation between test scores and honesty, civility, and civic responsibility are brushed aside. The impact of failure on children's psyches is declared an illusion. There is scant debate over what to do or how to do it. The charge to school principals and teachers is to just do it. (2002, p. 22)

The Problem

Describing the characteristics of successful schools is not difficult. The same descriptive traits found in the effective schools research of the 1970s continue to appear on lists of research-derived school effectiveness factors. The list below is derived from two syntheses of school effects research.

Characteristics of schools that consistently show good achievement gains:

- Strong academic leadership that produces consensus in goal priorities and commitment to excellence
- A safe, orderly school climate
- Positive teacher attitudes toward students and expectations regarding their abilities to master the curriculum
- An emphasis on objectives-based instruction in allocation of time and assignment of tasks to students
- Careful monitoring of progress toward goals through student testing and staff evaluation programs
- Strong parent involvement programs
- Consistent emphasis on the importance of achievement, including praise and public recognition for students' accomplishments

(Freiberg et al., 1990; Stringfield & Herman, 1996)

Despite all we know about schools that "work" and the waves of national and state attention to school reform, low achieving schools persist on the American landscape. Of course, public schools, in general, continue to provide a solid education for an extremely broad and diverse swath of children, and some schools sparkle as gems of excellence. More and more, the focus of concern is directed at a stubborn segment of the public school system which seems resistant to reform, comprehensive or otherwise. Low achieving schools are typically characterized as urban (or remotely rural), serving populations living in poverty, dealing with diversity of student readiness (including wide ranges of English language skills), and prone to categorization of students in ways that lower expectations (tracking and excessive classification and segregation for special education; Land & Legters, 2002). Operationally, low achieving schools tend to allow great discretion to teachers in "making up"

Public schools continue to provide a solid education for an extremely broad and diverse swath of children, and some schools sparkle as gems of excellence. More and more, the focus of concern is directed at a stubborn segment of the public school system which seems resistant to reform.

The Problem

instructional strategies without systematic regard for evidence-based practice, ongoing assessment of student learning, and alignment of instruction to intended outcomes (Slavin, 2002). Even with the common set of learning objectives provided by each state's learning standards and assessments, as required by No Child Left Behind and its predecessor legislation, instruction is still often characterized by haphazardness. This chaos is created, in part, by: a) the bewildering array of options teachers have for teaching (Rosenholtz, 1991); b) a school's lack of data on individual students with which teachers could base appropriate and timely remediation to improve achievement; c) the inability of school personnel to use data to the best advantage; and d) misunderstanding and misapplication of data in decision-making (Earl et al., 2002).

These characteristics of low achieving schools suggest the need for the kind of dramatic and thorough improvement that comprehensive school reform promises. The failure of comprehensive school reform to deliver on this promise is due, in large part, to the difficulty of fitting external models to particular school situations. When the square peg of the model meets the round hole of the school, something has to give. More often than not, the model is shaved to fit and loses its potency in the process. We might scan the deficiencies found in ineffective schools and conclude that they need:

- a system of alignment, data analysis, and targeted application of evidence-based instruction;
- systematic approaches to align actual classroom instruction with intended outcomes;
- convenient and accurate diagnostic feedback on student progress toward learning objectives; and
- solid grounding in evidence-based instructional practices and a systematic way to match strategies with diagnosed gaps in learning.

Pinpointing these specific areas for improvement, however, does not answer the question of why these schools are resistant to change. Such a narrow focus on curricular and instructional improvement fails to take into account the context in which instruction occurs and the systems, managerial and relational, that prevail in schools. In the years since comprehensive school reform was supported through federal initiatives, the percentage of schools adopting research-based CSR models has never been very large. Nationally, there was a decline in the percentage of eligible schools adopting CSR models from 20.2% in 1998 to 8.1% in 2002 (Viadero, 2004). Attempting to meet annual yearly progress as mandated by NCLB, most low-performing schools adopted hybrid reform approaches or clusters of projects and programs, often with inadequate understanding of their compatibility for the particular school context or their coherence within the school system.

In an ongoing study of the evolution of school improvement models by RAND, Susan Bodilly reports that ". . . designs changed over this time period [1992-1998] in several ways: planned development; response to the needs of students and teachers in the schools served; adaptation to conflicting policies, rules, and regulations; and complete reconceptualization of the design" (2001, p. 126). Planned development included changes to or the addition of a specific curriculum, processes for professional development of teachers, "cross-walking" the design's standards to a district's standards, and creation of diagnostic student assessments. Unplanned adaptations as a result of interactions with students and teachers included the necessity of creating basic literacy and numeracy programs; training teachers to adapt student assessment rubrics to state and district standards; and adjustments to the original design to account for the lack of teacher time and teacher capabilities. Existing policy environments of states, districts, schools, and unions caused the retooling of design components as the models scaled up. Timelines for implementation were lengthened, some design components were eliminated, and some required components became recommended. Bodilly concludes that:

> When teams allow mandated standards, assessments, curriculum, and other professional development to substitute for their own, the coherence of the school's program is possibly lessened or remains as fragmented as before the use of the design. Allowing a large range of implementation of elements of designs instead of strong adherence to design principles also increases the probability that the schools will never attempt the full vision of the design and never achieve the student performance hoped for by the design teams. (p. 127)

The Problem

Designs must be able to adapt to circumstances and change with experience, but guard against sacrificing their integrity in order to accommodate resistance and countervailing pressures inherent to school organizations. In the end, the model is judged by the results it produces. "Changes in the offerings and strategies of improvement programs can also wreak havoc on a school's efforts to implement and integrate initiatives. Although these changes often reflect the programs' efforts to increase their effectiveness, they may create confusion at the school level" (Hatch, 2002, p. 630).

The failure of a school reform model to deliver the expected results can be attributed to three causes, or a combination of the three: a) the prescribed practices are not sufficiently powerful to improve student achievement; b) the practices are not organized and presented in a manner that makes successful implementation likely; and c) the practices are not implemented well (Leithwood, Jantzi, & Mascall, 2002). Other obstacles to successful implementation of school improvement designs are the "presence of too many disconnected, episodic, piecemeal, superficially adorned projects" (Fullan, 2001, p. 109), and a tendency to negotiate down the requirements of the design in order to make it seem doable to the school (Hatch, 2002).

Prior to "comprehensive" school reform, a typical implementation mode involved the introduction of design strategies to a small cohort of teachers within a school, with the hope that their success would be contagious, and their expertise would be spread among their colleagues. In reality, some improvement efforts never grew beyond the original cohort, and some cohorts died on the vine. Comprehensive school reform called for whole-school change, and the importance of reaching an early critical mass of teacher buy-in and application became apparent. Robert Evans (1996) sums up the need for reaching a critical mass of support as follows:

> The ultimate goal may be a true schoolwide consensus for change, but the first and most crucial target is a critical mass of committed supporters. What is a critical mass? It depends on many factors and is impossible to quantify. It is the right number of the right people. In some situations this means a majority of the stakeholders, in others, a smaller number of respected, influential people. In either case, when innovation reaches this critical mass and has recruited a range of advocates, change acquires a momentum of its own and moves into the mainstream of discussion, perception, and practice. Much of the resistance that emerges in the early stages of implementation

CAUSES OF FAILURE

The failure of a school reform model to deliver the expected results can be attributed to three causes, or a combination of the three:

a) the prescribed practices are not sufficiently powerful to improve student achievement

b) the practices are not organized and presented in a manner that makes successful implementation likely

c) the practices are not implemented well

The Problem

begins to recede. Largely for this reason, the building of commitment among a critical mass of staff ranks among the most important goals change agents can set for themselves. (p. 69)

Evelyn Klein and Stefanie Bloom (2002), designers of programs to introduce science vocabulary in the early grades, draw a conclusion similar to Evans's from their experience in taking these programs to the field:

The most difficult component of the implementation of new programs is first persuading teachers to change their current practices to those determined to be most effective by the research community. Working directly with teachers to support implementation of an effective, validated, and research-based model of school reform, the authors learned that there is a critical need for increasing true teacher commitment for the use of such models in schools. (p. 9)

A Change in Course

A *model* is a template for operating a school that eliminates many possible courses of action in order to focus on one set of coherent actions. A model is typically designed by an external agency and adopted by a school. It provides an image of how things are to be. A school implements a model—puts it into place. For many schools, especially those where the possible courses of action are impossibly numerous and much effort is wasted sifting among them, a model is just what is needed. A model establishes a common vocabulary and standard practices; a model gives the school a mechanism for eliminating a lot of activity that does not fit the template. Think of the myriad of projects, programs, and events that grow like kudzu in a school over time. Often they begin to operate at cross purposes to one another, and resources of time and expertise do not allow for any of them to operate at a high level of quality. Ideally, a model is grounded in research and proven in the field.

So what could possibly be wrong with models as vehicles for school improvement? The primary problem with models is their inflexibility, on one hand, and the tendency to dilute their strengths on the other. Both of these limitations arise from the friction created when a fundamentally communal and personal institution takes on the raiment of cold management methodologies. And yet, scientific management has transformed industry into highly-efficient, exceptionally productive suppliers to match the demands of consumers. Will it do the same for schools? Only if the management models or systems can enhance rather than diminish the capacities and attachments of the people who inhabit schools—teachers, students, and the families who entrust their children to the schools.

Given the opportunity to implement a model, school personnel naturally expect to move toward a static vision of what that model represents. They ask to "see" what it will look like. Model providers distill from a thousand pieces of intricately-connected, research-based practice a set of principles from which can be molded something to show—a model. School personnel then view the model, without a full understanding of the many practices and their relationship to one another, and attempt to replicate it. Imagine looking at an automobile and then attempting to replicate it without an understanding of the functions and properties of its many parts. A school is no less complicated than a car.

DEFINITION

A ***model*** is a template for operating a school that eliminates many possible courses of action in order to focus on one set of coherent actions. A model is typically designed by an external agency and adopted by a school. It provides an image of how things are to be.

A Change in Course

The "professional development" approach to school improvement operates in the reverse direction from a model.

The "professional development" approach to school improvement operates in the reverse direction from a model. Over a period of time, school staff are "trained" in the myriad of research-based practices, typically in a hodge-podge of graduate courses, workshops, and institute days. No two teachers necessarily travel the same route and learn the same things. The pieces are unattached to one another. This approach is like disassembling an automobile and scattering the parts in several rooms, with a few teachers sent to each room to induce from the sampling of parts what the whole must be.

The logical remedy for the shortcomings of models and professional development approaches is to combine the two: Show the whole while also teaching the parts. In fact, this is what comprehensive school reform has attempted; model providers first demonstrate the efficacy of their prototype and then train school personnel to replicate it by studying its component parts, holding them to the light, shaking them, and learning how they work. While this dual-track strategy makes perfect sense and has been employed by model designers in comprehensive school reform, the results have not been impressive. Because school reform models are research-based, their faithful implementation should improve most schools. But faithful implementation is rare. The typical three-year implementation period passes through predictable phases of enthusiasm, frustration, resistance, softening of the model, and resigned submission to the inertia of the *status quo ante.* Then the implementation period ends, and atrophy begins. In fact, the deterioration of research-based practices adopted during the implementation period is often rapid or immediate. The same is true when administrators change, states mandate new directions, districts adopt new programs, or teachers leave and new ones arrive with no knowledge of the model.

Again, the problem is not in identifying the characteristics of effective schools; the problem is in moving schools in the direction of greater effectiveness. Change and sustainability are the challenges. For this reason, showing a school a "model" of what an ideal school might look like is only a very small first step in a long, never-ending journey to continuously improve student learning.

Theory to Practice

With its elegantly simple method of testing and revising theories by empirically examining their powers of prediction, science has nibbled away at the unknown for three hundred years, opening portals of light to an infinitely complex universe. Applying the same methods to the study of humankind, our development as distinct individuals, our relationships one to another, our institutions, cultures, and histories, social scientists, in just over a century, have advanced our understanding of ourselves. Natural science, in the wake of its discoveries, spawns technologies that alter the possibilities of human life, from medicines to computers to airplanes. Social science also creates technologies through its new understandings, and these technologies are found in public policy, human services, and education. Education, then, is an applied discipline which borrows from the social sciences the theories that are tested and revised.

As an applied social science—the inheritor of technologies spun off by psychology, sociology, economics, and political science—education is also a laboratory where the social sciences seek empirical verification for their theories. Public schools are enmeshed in the fabric of government and operate as polities in their own right, making them prime subjects for the inquiries of political scientists. Education is a sizeable segment of the economy, fueled largely by public dollars; schools prepare workers and consumers alike, and are economic systems with their own incentives and costs, all empirical opportunities for the theory-testing of economists. Psychological theories such as learning theory, motivation, behavior management, and efficacy are tested in schools, as are the sociological theories that find an ideal proving ground in an institution that so carefully groups its members and so meticulously accounts for their ethnicity and socioeconomic status.

Schools, then, are both the consumers of the technology spun off from social science and laboratories for testing the theories of social science. The process is circular, of course, with advances in theory leading to improvements in the technologies of teaching and learning. When a coherent set of theories is established and linked to a related system of practices (technologies), a model is born. A model is a system of practice rooted in a coherent set of theories. A model can itself be the object of further inquiry, as its efficacy and effectiveness are tested, giving evidence of the predictive potency of the underlying theories and the practical powers of its system of technologies. While education tends to borrow its theories from other disciplines, its philosophies are its own.

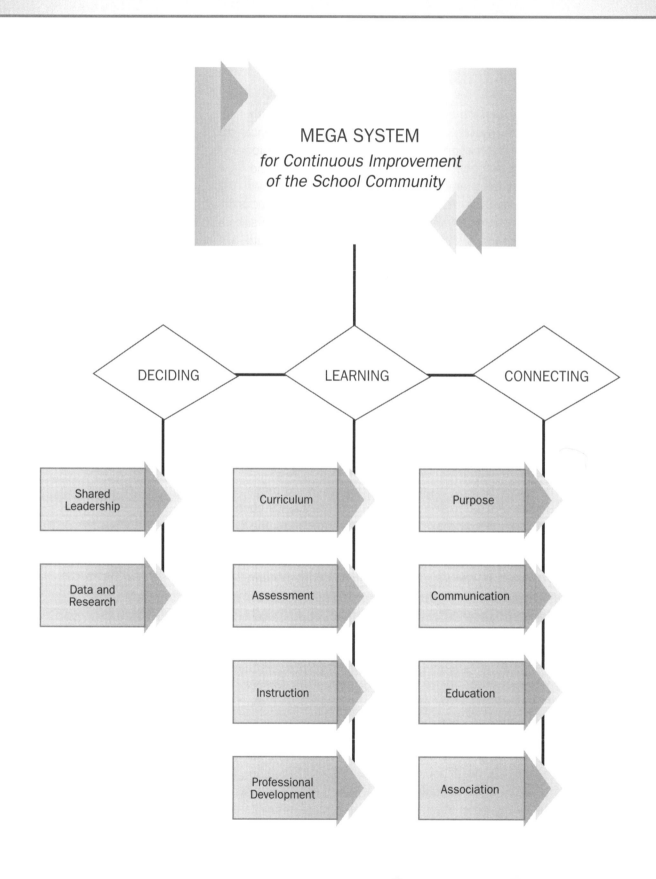

The Mega System

The Mega System reveals the Mega Project's experience with comprehensive school reform; thus, it seeks a workable balance among the school's internal and potentially sustainable decision-making structures and practices, sound teaching practices, and due regard for the human relationships that inhere to a place of community. The Mega System for school improvement is a blueprint for establishing a system of continuous improvement within a school. The process is informed by close attention to data. The ultimate measure of progress is student learning. The Mega System leans heavily on management methods, but places them in the hands of those responsible for the education of children in one school, with regard for all the idiosyncrasies that characterize any school and make it different from any other.

The word "process" is in disrepute among educationists these days, suffering from the connotation that it contrasts with "results," implying an emphasis on what teachers do rather than what students learn. Improved learning outcomes for students do not spring from closer scrutiny of data, however, but from the changes in instruction that scrutiny of data prompts. Student learning data is evidence of "results," and it is also feedback in a continuous "process" to improve the results. A school improvement process is not an endless trail of activity without fruition, but a chain in which each link contains "results" that strengthen the next link and, consequentially, the chain itself.

Continuous school improvement is, in essence, an engineering function. A good engineer knows enough basic research to make informed decisions, and closely examines data to make the right adjustments in a system to produce the best results. The engineer also knows when to call on the researcher for guidance, when to listen to the frontline users of the product, and how to understand each part of the system in relationship to the whole. The Mega System places teams in the role of engineers, constantly tweaking the parts of the system to make a more effective whole.

The Mega System is composed of three parts: Deciding, Learning, and Connecting. These parts, bound together coherently, are an attempt to marry the efficiencies of management theory (decision-making) with the art of good teaching (learning), in due tribute to the essential relationships (connections) among a school's constituents. Deciding includes the structures and processes for decision-making, including shared leadership, use of timely data, and attention to research. Learning encompasses curriculum (what is taught), assessment (knowing what is mastered), instruction (the way learning is organized), and professional development (building the expertise of school staff). Connecting is the bridge-building component, which is also a means of promoting a sense of community, and attends to the articulation of core values about education, the engagement of parents, and communication and mutual support among teachers, students, parents, and school staff. The next three chapters cover the three parts of the Mega System.

Putting a System in Place

Putting in place a system for continuous improvement is not the same as replicating a model. Let's review a few points made in this chapter. We said that after experience with comprehensive school reform models, our conclusion is that we need to: a) replace the static model with a system of continuous improvement; b) abandon the replication of a prototype and chase the lodestar of student success; and c) swap allegiance to implementation for the corrective powers of timely data and sound research. High-functioning schools and schools cited for their "effectiveness" do the right things, do them well continuously, and always look for ways to improve. Dramatically changing the way a school operates when the school is not functioning well, as comprehensive school reform attempts to do, takes time beyond the ordinary, an infusion of *new* time into a time-scarce system. Schools that fail with comprehensive school reform do so not for lack of resources, other than time, but for want of determination and internal discipline. In some cases, the model is not appropriate for the school, but in most cases the model is compromised, not to make a productive fit with the school, but in incremental defeats in the face of opposition and difficulty. The same can happen with a "system" of improvement, unless its guardians remember that the system must flex and bend only in response to evidence of changes in student learning. Student success, as evidenced in learning outcomes, must be the lodestar.

That said, the first elements of the system to put in place are: a) decision-making structures to monitor progress and alter practices to achieve the best results, and b) data processes that provide

The Mega System

frequent and reliable measures of student learning and operational information. Once the decision-making structures and the data collection processes are in place, changes in curriculum and instruction can proceed. The next chapter describes decision-making and data processes that establish the foundation for a system of continuous school improvement. Subsequent chapters add detail about learning and about connections within the school community. Each chapter includes checklists of indicators to guide school-based teams in determining the completeness of the system for continuous improvement. Beyond that, the teams will establish their own methods for examining the effectiveness of the system to produce improved results in student learning. The teams will also develop specific measures to determine the effectiveness of each part in the system and their relationship to the whole.

Where to begin? The Leadership Team described in the next chapter can use the checklists of indicators provided in each chapter as a needs assessment, determining which parts of the ultimate system for continuous improvement are in place and which parts must be added. If there is no Leadership Team, establishing one may be the first order of business. From the needs assessment derived from the indicator checklists, a "school improvement system plan" can be developed, outlining the components of the system that must be added or improved, timelines, and teams or persons responsible. The indicator checklists can be used periodically to reassess the health of the system.

Chapter 1 References

Berliner, D. C., & Biddle, B. J. (1995). *The manufactured crisis: Myths, fraud, and the attack on America's schools.* Reading, MA: Addison-Wesley.

Berends, M., Bodilly, S. J., & Kirby, S. N. (2002). *Facing the challenges of whole-school reform.* Santa Monica, CA: RAND.

Bodilly, S. (2001). *New American Schools' concept of break the mold designs.* Santa Monica, CA: RAND.

Borman, G. D. (2005). National efforts to bring reform to scale in high-poverty schools: Outcomes and implications. In L. Parker (Ed.), *Review of research in education, 29* (pp. 1-27). Washington, DC: American Educational Research Association.

Chall, J. S. (2000). *The academic achievement challenge: What really works in the classroom.* New York: Guilford Press.

Coleman, J. S., et al. (1966). *Equality of educational opportunity.* Washington, DC: Office of Education.

Coleman, J. S. (1981). *Longitudinal data analysis.* New York: Basic Books.

Coleman, J. S. (1987, August-September). Families and schools. *Educational Researcher*, 36-37.

Coleman, J. S., & Hoffer, T. (1987). *Public and private high schools: The impact of communities.* New York: Basic Books.

Deming, W. E. (1986). *Out of the crisis.* Cambridge: MIT Press.

Earl, L., Watson, N., & Torrance, N. (2002). *Front row seats: What we've learned from the national literacy and numeracy strategies in England.* Paper presented at the annual meeting of the American Educational Research Association, New Orleans, LA.

Edmonds, R. (1979, October). Effective schools for the urban poor. *Educational Leadership, 37*(1), 15-24.

Evans, R. (1996). *The human side of school change.* San Francisco: Jossey-Bass.

Freiberg, H., Prokosch, N., Treister, E., & Stein, T. (1990). Turning around five at-risk elementary schools. *School Effectiveness and School Improvement, 1,* 5-25.

Fullan, M. (2001). *Leading in a culture of change.* San Francisco: Jossey-Bass.

Goodlad, J. I. (2002). Kudzu, rabbits, and school reform. *Phi Delta Kappan, 84*(1), 16-23.

Hatch, T. (2002, April). When improvement programs collide. *Phi Delta Kappan, 83*(8), 626-634, 639.

Hanushek, E., et al. (1994). *Making schools work.* Washington, DC: The Brookings Institution.

Hirsch, Jr., E. D. (2001). The roots of the education wars. In T. Loveless (Ed.), *The great curriculum debate* (pp. 13-24). Washington, DC: The Brookings Institution.

Klein, E. R., & Bloom, S. F. (2002). *School reform programs: Reforming educators' willingness to use them*. Philadelphia: Laboratory for Student Success.

Land, D., & Letgers, N. (2002). The extent and consequences of risk in U. S. education. In S. Stringfield & D. Land (Eds.), *Educating at-risk students* (pp. 1-28). Chicago: University of Chicago Press.

Leithwood, K., Jantzi, D., & Mascall, B. (2002). *A framework for research on large-scale reform.* Paper presented at the annual meeting of the American Educational Research Association, New Orleans, LA.

National Commission on Excellence in Education. (1983). *A nation at risk: The imperative for educational reform*. Washington, DC: U.S. Government Printing Office.

Ravitch, D. (2000). *Left back: A century of failed school reforms*. New York: Simon & Schuster.

Rosenholtz, S. (1991). *Teacher's workplace*. New York: Teacher's College Press.

Shavelson, R. J., & Towne, L. (Eds.). (2002). *Scientific research in education*. Washington, DC: National Academy Press.

Sergiovanni, T. (1999). *Building community in schools*. San Francisco: Jossey-Bass.

Slavin, R. (2002). The intentional school: Effective elementary education for all children. In S. Stringfield & D. Land (Eds.), *Educating at-risk students* (pp. 111-127). Chicago: University of Chicago Press.

Stringfield, S., & Herman, R. (1996). Assessment of the state of school effectiveness research in the United States of America. *School Effectiveness and School Improvement, 7*(2), 159-180.

Viadero, D. (2004, April 21) Reform programs backed by research find fewer takers. *Education Week*. Retrieved April 22, 2004, from http://www.edweek.org.

Deciding—The Executive Function

Decision-making in schools is both shared and hierarchical. The idea of "shared leadership" is that leaders make decisions, and some decisions are best made by folks playing a variety of roles in a school community. To share leadership is to distribute decision-making among the constituencies of the school community, to place decision-making in the appropriate hands rather than to embed it within an organizational position. A desired consequence of shared leadership is to make the school community immune to the disruptions caused by changes in personnel, to provide continuity in the pursuit of goals, and internalization of values, purpose, and practice. Shared leadership contributes to a distinct school culture, broad understanding of and participation in the school's direction, and access to all the human and social capital that reside within the school community.

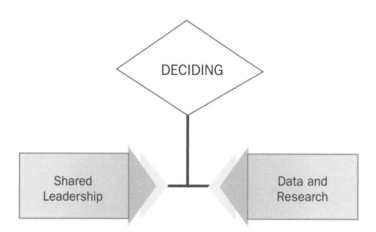

Today, states make the ultimate decision about what students should know and when they should know it, at least at the level of minimum expectation expressed as learning standards. Districts make decisions about the basic materials and other resources available to the teacher and the general conditions under which they teach. Districts also flesh out the state's content standards with their own curriculum guides. Districts and schools together decide how to sort students into programmatic categories, how to cluster and place them. Within the borders of these hierarchical determinations, teachers and their instructional leaders are best equipped to design the instructional process, form and refine specific learning objectives, establish criteria for mastery, plan learning activities, and monitor student learning day to day. To accomplish this requires time for teachers to meet, discipline to stay on course, and external standards to mark their effectiveness. Data-based decision-making (DBDM) includes schedules for teacher collaboration, guidelines for their productivity, and encouragement for them to tap and pool their individual talents. A team structure meets these purposes, again hierarchically, with a leadership team tending to the overall functioning of the system and the continuous improvement of the school, and instructional teams building and monitoring the basic units of instruction. To focus on the engagement of parents in student's learning, a third type of team includes parents along with teachers.

Computers, databases, software-based management systems, the internet, instructional software, e-mail, and technology-based modes of presentation are tools that make DBDM efficient. They help put the right information in the right place at the right time. They are not the information itself, but a means for organizing, presenting, and analyzing the information.

The Mega System describes three interrelated aspects of decision-making—shared leadership, data, and research. Like the good engineer, those charged with managing and improving a school's "system" know when to call on researchers for guidance, when to listen to the various constituents within the system (teachers, students, parents), how to understand each part of the system in relationship to the whole, and what data to examine to inform their decisions.

ASPECTS OF DECISION-MAKING

The Mega System describes three interrelated aspects of decision-making—shared leadership, data, and research.

Shared Leadership

LEADERSHIP CHARACTERISTICS

Three leader characteristics critical to building personal relationships that are conducive to effective reform efforts:

1) optimism
2) honesty
3) consideration

Leadership could be considered the single most important aspect of effective school reform.

Robert Marzano (2003)

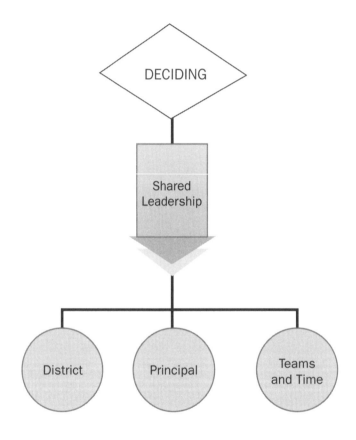

Robert Marzano (2003) points to leadership as the *sine quo non* of school improvement. "Leadership," he writes, "could be considered the single most important aspect of effective school reform" (p. 172). Wherever leadership resides—with the principal, team leaders, committee chairs, or central office staff—some personal characteristics are associated with effectiveness in school improvement. As a result of their survey of more than 1,200 K-12 teachers, Blasé and Kirby (2000) identified three leader characteristics as critical to building personal relationships that are conducive to effective reform efforts: 1) optimism, 2) honesty, and 3) consideration. Optimism provides hope during the difficult times that inevitably come with change initiatives. It is defined as the power of nonnegative thinking. The leader acknowledges obstacles but does not portray them as insurmountable. Honesty is characterized by truthfulness, but also by a congruence between words and actions. To sustain a change effort, teachers and parents must have a sense that what they are told is accurate and that there are no important things occurring about which they are not

Shared Leadership

informed. Consideration is a trait that refers to "people orientation" or a concern for people. Blasé and Kirby note that "considerate principals were viewed as non-discriminating; they show concern for all teachers. They express interest in their teachers' lives during both happy and sad events" (p. 110). It might be said that these characteristics, which are such crucial components of school climate, are as important as the more technical aspects of school improvement.

As the conductor of culture, the principal attends to both the human elements of the school community and the organization's pursuit of goals. "The new culture of schools should encourage and expect that a leader will orchestrate a program that includes measurable goals, as well as regular praise and celebration of progress towards those goals" (Schmoker, 1996, p. 105). This mixture of personal support for all the players and focused attention to systemic goals, especially improved learning, is a balanced view of leadership. Marzano advocates for a strong instructional leadership *team* consisting of the principal and a dedicated group of classroom teachers who work together on curriculum and instruction issues. This leadership team also serves as a conduit for communication, ensuring that the views and concerns of all members of the school faculty are represented in decisions. It is his view that "leadership for change is most effective when carried out by a small group of educators with the principal functioning as a strong cohesive force" (p. 174).

The efficacy of team leadership is touted by other education scholars as a means to effectively share leadership and achieve organizational goals. The effective principal works with a school leadership team, sometimes called a site management or learning support team, (Lambert, 2003), to structure school improvement conversations based on the investigation of data that describes present and desired student achievement. Out of this analysis comes goal-setting for the school. Schmoker (1996) encourages schools to set small, measurable goals that can be achieved monthly, quarterly, or annually. Small, measurable successes are the seeds of large-scale success, and can release optimism and enthusiasm, or "zest" as Schaffer (1988, p. 52) calls it. A teaching staff can use this zest to maintain energy for reaching further goals. "Immediate success is essential if people are to increase their confidence and expand their vision of what is possible" (Schaffer, 1988, p. 60). So, a principal's task is to help the instructional staff focus the goals for both short-term and long-term student achievement. In so doing, the principal also demonstrates skills that help build leadership capacity among teachers.

School personnel—teachers, support staff, parent leaders—like everyone else, respond to sincere praise, public recognition, and reward or celebration of accomplishment, both individual and team. The balanced coupling of clear expectations with recognition for accomplishment is essential to effective school leadership (Blasé & Kirby, 1992; Evans, 1993; Lortie, 1975). Leaders who understand motivation know that success and improvement are "every bit as social as they are structural" (Schmoker, 1996, p. 104).

Immediate success is essential if people are to increase their confidence and expand their vision of what is possible.

(Schaffer, 1988, p. 60)

Starting at the Top: The District Connection

Most schools are members of districts or other such larger organizations, and so clarification is needed about which decisions are made at the district level and which decisions are made within the school. The Mega System for continuous school improvement begins when the district and the school construct a letter of understanding. A school is not an island unto itself. District policies and support affect a school's ability to initiate and sustain a system of continuous improvement. Many attempts at school reform have gone awry when the well-intentioned initiatives of the district compete with the earnest efforts of the school for time, resources, and allegiance. The district is most helpful to a school's continuous improvement when:

- The superintendent regularly reports to the school board the progress of individual schools, and each school regularly reports and documents its progress.

- The district designates a central office contact person for the school, and that person maintains close communication with the school and an interest in its progress.

- District policies and procedures support site-based decision-making and clarify the scope of decision-making granted the school.

- District and school decision-makers meet regularly (at least once a month) to discuss the school's progress.

- The district has translated national and state standards/expectations into a cohesive district curriculum.

- Staff development is built into the school schedule by the district, but the school is allowed discretion in selecting training and consultation that fit its current needs.

- Staff development is offered to support staff (e.g., aides, clerks, custodians, cooks) as well as classroom teachers.

Shared Leadership

- The district provides the technology, training, and support
to facilitate the school's data management needs.

A letter of understanding between the central office/district and
the school addresses the items listed above and related matters.

The Principal

The principal's role is not only to share leadership, but to build the
leadership capacity of others in the school. The principal provides the
organizational attention to the school's teams to keep them focused
and productive. The principal is the guardian of sound practice and
challenger of questionable teaching, but also teaches and encourages
others to do the same. The principal is the scheduler and convener,
making it possible for teams of decision-makers to meet and perform.
The principal is the executor of plans laid by decision-making teams.
The principal, most of all, takes time (at least half of the principal's
time) helping teachers improve their teaching. The effective principal
helps everyone in the school maintain focus and energy in continuously
improving student learning. To do that, the principal sets short-
term objectives leading to longer-term goals, builds the leadership
capacity of teachers, staff, and parents, facilitates the operation of
decision-making and work-producing teams, and provides regular and
timely recognition, reinforcement, and reward, including celebration
for goal attainment. Big job. Sharing leadership is hard work.

The principal, of course, is the "chief" leader in the school, by
virtue of organizational position, so the sharing begins with the
principal reassessing the nature of that position. This is not always
an easy assignment. Depending upon the era in which the principal
was trained for the position, the nature of the job was described by
graduate school professors in ways that do not necessarily fit well
with shared leadership. The position of principal has traditionally
been described in purely managerial and bureaucratic terms, one of
the hierarchy in "school administration." Bus schedules, budgets,
building maintenance, and careful adherence to the intricate statutes
and procedural guidelines of public education were paramount. By the
1980s, the principal's role was taking on a human resources dimension
that was, while still managerial in its conception, more attentive
to the human capital that resides in the teaching faculty (Flanigan,
1990). More recently, the principal has been portrayed as the fire
carrier for the school's vision, the central character in instructional
planning, and a collaborator who brought teachers and even parents
into discussions about the school's operation (Lambert, 2003).

The principal's role is not
only to share leadership,
but to build the leadership
capacity of others in the
school.

With the rise of accountability, the principal's role took on a sharper focus—get results. Getting results meant improving test scores. Placing the emphasis on test scores turned the manager into a reformer, and reform was first sought through "restructuring." Enthusiasm for restructuring abounded. Sashkin and Egermeier (1993) believed that a focus on accountability and the restructuring necessary to get results would make the technical skills and knowledge of the principal highly valued. Restructuring, they wrote, "involves changes in roles, rules, and relationships between and among students and teachers, teachers and administrators, and administrators at various levels from the school building to the district office to the state level, all with the aim of improving student outcomes" (p. 14).

One of the common misconceptions about leadership at the school level is that it should reside with one individual—namely the principal.

Marzano (2003)

Others, including Michael Fullan (1993), are less enthusiastic, calling restructuring "tinkering," when what public education needed was "reculturing." "Reculturing involves changing the norms, values, incentives, skills, and relationships in the organization to foster a different way of working together. Reculturing *does* make a difference in teaching and learning" (p. 9). Schlechty (1990) also agrees that the task for schools of the future is reculturing:

> Social structures are embedded in systems of meaning, value, belief, and knowledge; such systems comprise the culture of an organization. To change an organization's structure, therefore, one must attend not only to rules, roles, and relationships but to systems of beliefs, values, and knowledge as well. Structural change requires cultural change. (pp. xvi-xvii)

Much is expected of principals today. They are expected often to disregard their own professional training and adopt new definitions of their role. How, then, is the principal to know what is fad and what is essential? In fact, as new tasks for the principal are emphasized, old ones are not eliminated. While the principal may now be expected to restructure, reculture, and reform, she must still see that the buses run on time, the gym floor gets waxed, and the pop machines are filled.

Saying that the principal is the "instructional leader" of the school has become cliché. What exactly does it mean? Marzano (2003) points out that "one of the common misconceptions about leadership at the school level is that it should reside with one individual—namely the principal" (p. 174). It seems, however, that one aspect of the contemporary principalship is not disputed: The principal is the

Shared Leadership

focus keeper, consistently pointing to improved student learning as the central objective of the school. With that understood, leadership is shared among teachers, support staff, parents, and, in some cases, the students themselves in order to achieve that objective. In addition to setting the climate of high expectations for student achievement, Marzano explains that "effective leadership for change is characterized by specific behaviors that enhance interpersonal relationships" (p. 176). Helping teams function effectively is part of this important aspect of the principal's job.

Teams and Time

Leadership within the school requires *teams* and *time*. That is, decision-making groups must be organized and given time to plan and monitor the parts of the system for which they are responsible. This is an immense challenge in most schools, where teachers are available for very little time beyond the hours for which they are responsible for teaching and supervising students. Finding time for a group of teachers to meet is not easy, but it is essential. Different groups or teams of school personnel have different needs for the amount and distribution of time required for them to attend to their responsibilities. Guidelines are provided below for the minimum amount of meeting and planning time required for each team. Additional time is needed for professional development.

The Leadership Team

Some decisions concern the general operation of the school and its continuous improvement. The Mega System places those decisions with a Leadership Team that is headed by the principal and includes teachers and other staff. In order to facilitate communication and coordination among the grade levels and departments of the school, a typical composition of the Leadership Team is the principal and team leaders from the Instructional Teams. The Leadership Team needs to meet twice each month for an hour each meeting. Less frequent meetings lead to drift and loss of continuity; less time for each meeting creates hurriedness and insufficient attention to the work at hand. Effective teams operate with agendas, keep minutes, stay focused, and follow through with the plans they make.

> Leadership within the school requires *teams* and *time*. That is, decision-making groups must be organized and given time to plan and monitor the parts of the system for which they are responsible.

Shared Leadership

PURPOSES

Instructional Teams need time for two purposes:

1) meetings
2) curricular and instructional planning

Instructional Teams

Some decisions are best made by the teachers responsible for particular groups of students—grade level teams or subject area teams, which we will call "instructional teams." Instructional Teams are manageable groupings of teachers by grade level or subject area who meet to develop instructional strategies aligned to the standards-based curriculum and to monitor the progress of the students in the grade levels or subject area for which the team is responsible. Instructional Teams need time for two purposes: 1) meetings, and 2) curricular and instructional planning. A 45-minute meeting twice a month is ideal for maintaining communication and organizing the work at hand, operating with agendas, minutes, and focus. In addition, a block of 4 to 6 hours of time once a month is necessary for curricular and instructional planning, and additional whole days before and after the school year are a great advantage.

School Community Council

A third category of decisions addresses the community of the school—administrators, staff, teachers, students, parents, and volunteers—and focuses on the areas of overlapping responsibility among these people, their relationships to one another, and their allegiance to common educational values. We suggest a "school community council" (SCC) with the principal, counselor, social worker, teachers, and parents as the majority of members. The SCC meets twice each month for an hour each meeting. Because the SCC is a planning or steering committee, it has no staff to carry out its plans. The school designates a professional staff person as "parent education facilitator" to help execute the plans of the SCC alongside the principal. The Parent Education Facilitator typically receives a stipend for assuming these extra duties. Like the other teams, the SCC knows its scope of responsibility and operates with agendas, minutes, and focus.

Use of Data and Research

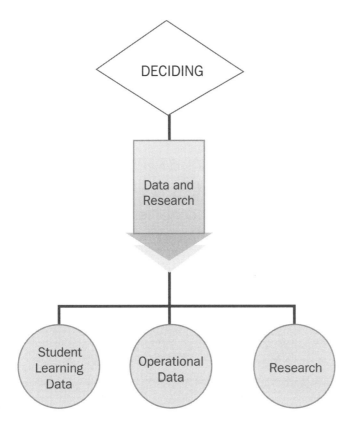

Information. A teacher can have too little of it or too much of it. A team can spend too much time raking through information that yields no helpful understanding. Timely, pertinent information (data) is necessary to team decision-making and to teacher decision-making. The school improvement plan is the central and coordinating document for organizing information and making good decisions. We distinguish among three types of information: 1) student learning data, which tells teams and teachers what students know and can do; 2) operational data, which tells teams how the system and subsystems are functioning, and how the school improvement plan is being carried out; and 3) research, the evidence gathered from outside the system from the study of published education literature, visits to other schools, and participation in education conferences. Teams, in analyzing both operational and student learning data, in fact, conduct their own research, which also informs the system.

Student Learning Data

Within each school on any given day, teachers make thousands of decisions that, in their aggregate, determine the school's effectiveness in advancing its students' learning. These decisions are made in real time, on the fly, as teachers mix the inflowing flood of data from their classroom with their own mental storehouse of content knowledge, tactical options, and seasoned savvy to respond to a student's question, interpret a student's expression, or assess a student's work. These decision points are measured in microseconds, their calculation never recorded, their consequences immense. The mind of the teacher, what we call "human capital," that reservoir holding years of training and experience, is a school's principal asset.

> The mind of the teacher, what we call "human capital," that reservoir holding years of training and experience, is a school's principal asset.

Data-based decision-making (DBDM) is a companion to the teacher's mental artistry, and it serves two purposes: 1) to stock the teacher's pool of knowledge, and 2) to reduce the teacher's chance of error. Beginning at the essential nexus of teacher-student-content, data (reliable information) help the teacher answer the question: What does a student know? A well-structured system of data analysis places in a teacher's hands (indeed, in her head) maps with boundaries, limiting the field of the unknown. What do we expect a student to know? What does a student know? What teaching strategies will best serve this student?

PURPOSES OF DBDM

Data-based decision-making (DBDM) is a companion to the teacher's mental artistry, and it serves two purposes:

1) to stock the teacher's pool of knowledge

2) to reduce the teacher's chance of error

State learning standards and their grade-level benchmarks, when sufficiently explicit and rigorous, in part answer the question "What do we expect a student to know?" State assessments based on these standards provide some evidence of what a student knows. But standards and state assessments are far removed from the daily decision-making of classroom teachers. Standards are also better at establishing a floor of expectation for all students than in opening the doors of possibility for a particular student. The school's own system of data-based decision-making helps fill this gap, netting together the various levels of curriculum content, instructional strategy, individual student mastery, and individual student potentiality.

A good DBDM system harnesses the human capital held by teachers, organizes information for the teacher, monitors the teacher's practices, and engages the teacher in the continuous improvement of the system itself. For this reason, a DBDM system is more than the information it holds; it is also the structures and processes of decision-making that include the teacher at their center.

Use of Data and Research

Alignment of Standards, Curriculum, Assessment, and Instruction

Schools have invested heavily in curriculum alignment, mapping their curricula to standards, benchmarks, and specific items of standards-based assessment. The resulting alignment is a set of data, a body of information carefully organized, that helps answer the question "What do we expect a student to know?" The challenge that lies ahead for most schools is to draw further connections between the aligned curriculum, the taught curriculum, the most efficacious instructional strategies, and the mastery evidenced by the individual student. This must be done in a way that ensures that all students achieve the expected level of mastery while allowing each student ample opportunity to soar beyond that minimum expectation. The linkage from curriculum to instruction is tenuous in many schools, and insufficient systems are in place for capturing information about what is taught, how it is taught, and how it might best be learned by an individual student.

Instructional Practices

The research literature provides a wealth of information on instructional practices, but the usefulness of this information cannot be assumed from its abundance. Matching particular practices to the subject area, grade level, and students' prior learning can be a massive undertaking, leaving too much unproductive chaff in the bushel of productive grain. In the end, the teacher must hit the target where content, instructional mode, and learner requisites optimally meet. A DBDM system can help a teacher hit the target. Monitoring the application of targeted learning strategies by teachers can help a school refine its professional development processes and improve its teachers' effectiveness.

Operational Data

Operational data helps the Leadership Team monitor the functioning of the school's systems. Operational data include:

- **Documents** such as the school's policies and procedures, schedule, programs, and improvement plans;
- **Evaluations** of the school's programs;
- **Observational data** collected from classroom observations;

· **Perceptions data** such as surveys of teachers', parents', and students' perceptions about the school; and

· **Proceedings of teams**, including their agendas, minutes, and work products.

The school improvement plan is a good beginning point to establish coherent streams of data to facilitate decision-making. For example, the school improvement plan might include an objective to improve reading achievement by adopting a strategy of reading across the curriculum. Professional development will be provided for teachers to improve their skills in teaching reading across the curriculum. Was the training provided? Who attended? How did the participants evaluate the effectiveness of the training? Do minutes of Instructional Team meetings show that teams carried the training into their discussions and plans? How does the school assess the degree to which teachers changed practices as a result of the training? How does the school determine the effectiveness of the changed practices? Putting all these pieces together depends upon first instituting standard practices and procedures that: (a) link the improvement plan to subsequent activities, such as professional development; (b) maintain records of participation in trainings; (c) gather participant evaluations of trainings; (d) require minutes of team meetings; (e) gather information from individual teachers on changed practices; (f) gather information about short-term effectiveness of changed practices, such as teacher ratings; and (g) determine improvements in student learning that might result from particular changes in practice.

While each of these procedures might be in place, a more common problem is that each is carried out in isolation from the others. Only by bringing the data together, succinctly, in one report or a coordinated set of reports can the Leadership Team put the pieces together and judge the merits of the undertaking. This can be managed by developing for each item in the school improvement plan a brief flow chart that links together the information that will be necessary to make sound decisions about that item. The team might then designate a team member to follow through, collect the information, and prepare a succinct report. In this way, each Leadership Team member shares a piece of the data collection chores, and the team is able to make decisions from sound and focused information.

Use of Data and Research

Research

A good school improvement plan links each of its objectives to evidence of its appropriateness to the situation, its potential efficacy, and its predicted results. In other words, the plan begins on firm footing. The search for evidence begins not with the objective, however, but with the problem that gave rise to the objective. Continuous improvement is a cycle of trying and testing, trying and testing. Each test of an intervention invariably produces a mixed-bag of results, and the difficulties and disappointments become problem statements for new attempts at refinement or replacement of the intervention. Each problem statement requires a review of the research literature. Visiting schools to see, first-hand, how a possible intervention might work is part of the research. Conversations with teachers and administrators from other schools might serve the same purpose. Once the evidence has been gathered, a menu of research-based options is produced. The team selects from this menu, creates an objective and a plan to achieve it, determines the criteria for measuring the success of the plan, and collects the information necessary for making sound judgments.

Having the research conveniently at hand is essential. A file is created for each section of the school improvement plan, and as administrators and teachers find articles pertinent to that section, the articles are placed in the file. When staff members attend professional conferences, they return with satchels of documents that can be culled to select the most convincing evidence to be placed in the research file. Then when an objective is set or modified, or a new problem is detected, the research file provides a starting point to select sound options. The research file should be kept in a place where it is accessible to teachers but can also be kept organized and circulation monitored. The library or school office may be such a place, with someone assigned to maintain the file.

Chapter Summary

Shared leadership requires the appropriate distribution of decision-making among the constituencies of the school community; attention to the human element; the internalization of values, purpose, and practice within a distinct school culture; and business-like proceedings of the various teams. When leadership is shared, the leadership capacity of all the participants must be nurtured. Time for decision-making is essential. While organizing teams and distributing decision-making among them is a structural first step, the principal retains a central role in coordinating the teams' activities, maintaining focus on the school's goals, and fostering a culture in which values, purpose, and practices are embedded and not dependent upon the particular players who occupy roles in the school community.

Making good decisions depends upon access to timely and pertinent information—data and research. The principal serves as the keeper of a system of data collection, organization, and presentation, with each team playing its part in the process. Data fall into two categories—student learning data and operational data. Research is tied to identified directions and problems which are often expressed in the school improvement plan.

Putting Decision-Making Components in Place

The forms on the following pages may be used to assess the current status of key elements of a decision-making system and to plan for the development of the missing pieces. A Leadership Team can work through these forms, develop a plan of action, and monitor the progress. For items checked "No" on the assessment of the current situation, primary responsibility is assigned to a person or team, with an expected date for completion of the task.

Decision-Making Indicators

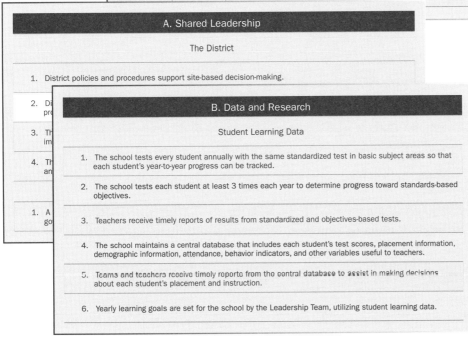

Assessing the Current Situation		Adding the Missing Pieces	
Yes	No	Primary Responsibility	Target Date for Completion

A. Shared Leadership

The District

1. District policies and procedures support site-based decision-making.

2. Di__
    pr__

3. Th__
    im__

4. Th__
    an__

1. A__
    go__

B. Data and Research

Student Learning Data

1. The school tests every student annually with the same standardized test in basic subject areas so that each student's year-to-year progress can be tracked.

2. The school tests each student at least 3 times each year to determine progress toward standards-based objectives.

3. Teachers receive timely reports of results from standardized and objectives-based tests.

4. The school maintains a central database that includes each student's test scores, placement information, demographic information, attendance, behavior indicators, and other variables useful to teachers.

5. Teams and teachers receive timely reports from the central database to assist in making decisions about each student's placement and instruction.

6. Yearly learning goals are set for the school by the Leadership Team, utilizing student learning data.

Decision-Making Indicators

A. Shared Leadership

The District

1. District policies and procedures support site-based decision-making.

2. District and school decision-makers are connected by frequent interaction, two-way communication, problem solving, mutual coordination, and reciprocal influence.

3. The district has provided the school with a "letter of understanding" about the school's continuous improvement system and the district's support for it.

4. The district has assigned a contact person for the school to serve as a liaison between the central office and the school to advance the school's continuous improvement.

Teams and Time

1. A team structure is officially incorporated into the school improvement plan and school governance policy.

2. A Leadership Team including the principal and teacher leaders from each Instructional Team is in place.

3. The Leadership Team meets regularly (twice a month or more).

4. The Leadership Team seeks the input of others not on the team, in order to represent all faculty/staff.

5. The Leadership Team serves as a conduit of communication to the faculty and staff.

6. The Leadership Team shares in decisions of real substance pertaining to curriculum, instruction, assessment, and professional development.

7. The Leadership Team regularly looks at school performance data and uses that data to make decisions about school improvement needs.

8. Teachers are organized into grade-level, grade-level cluster, or subject-area Instructional Teams.

9. Instructional Teams meet regularly (twice a month or more) to conduct business.

10. Instructional Teams meet for blocks of time sufficient to develop and refine units of instruction and review student learning data.

11. A School Community Council including the principal, teacher representative(s), counselor, parent liaison, and parents is in place.

| Assessing the Current Situation | | Adding the Missing Pieces | | |
Yes	No	Primary Responsibility		Target Date for Completion

Decision-Making Indicators

A. Shared Leadership *(continued)*	
Teams and Time	
12. A majority of the members of the SCC are parents of currently enrolled students who are not also employees of the school.	
13. The SCC meets regularly (twice a month or more).	
14. The SCC is organized with a constitution and by-laws.	
15. All teams prepare agendas for their meetings.	
16. All teams maintain official minutes of their meetings.	
17. The principal maintains a file of the agendas, work products, and minutes of all teams.	
The Principal	
1. Principal makes sure everyone understands the school's mission, clear goals, and their roles in meeting the goals.	
2. Principal leads and participates actively with the Leadership Team.	
3. Principal participates actively with the SCC and shows support for its significance.	
4. Principal monitors the work of the Instructional Teams and helps to keep them focused on instructional improvement.	
5. Principal monitors curriculum and classroom instruction regularly.	
6. Principal helps poorly performing teachers to improve.	
7. Principal spends at least 50% of his/her time working directly with teachers to improve instruction.	

Assessing the Current Situation		Adding the Missing Pieces	
Yes	No	Primary Responsibility	Target Date for Completion

Decision-Making Indicators

B. Data and Research	
Student Learning Data	
1. The school tests every student annually with the same achievement test in basic subject areas so that each student's year-to-year progress can be tracked.	
2. The school tests each student at least 3 times each year to determine progress toward standards-based objectives.	
3. Teachers receive timely reports of results from periodic, standards-aligned tests.	
4. The school maintains a central database that includes each student's test scores, placement information, demographic information, attendance, behavior indicators, and other variables useful to teachers.	
5. Teams and teachers receive timely reports from the central database to assist in making decisions about each student's placement and instruction.	
6. Yearly learning goals are set for the school by the Leadership Team, utilizing student learning data.	
7. The Leadership Team monitors school-level student learning data.	
8. Instructional Teams use student learning data to assess strengths and weaknesses of the curriculum.	
9. Instructional Teams use student learning data to plan instruction.	
10. Instructional Teams use student learning data to identify students in need of instructional support or enhancement.	
11. Instructional Teams review the results of unit pre-/post-tests to make decisions about the curriculum and instructional plans.	
Operational Data	
1. The Leadership Team maintains an accessible file of key documents including the school improvement plan, policies and procedures, schedules, and program descriptions.	
2. The Leadership Team maintains an accessible file of evaluations of the school's programs.	
3. The principal compiles reports from classroom observations, showing aggregate areas of strength and areas that need improvement without revealing the identity of individual teachers.	
4. The Leadership Team reviews the principal's summary reports of classroom observations and takes them into account in planning professional development.	

	Assessing the Current Situation		Adding the Missing Pieces	
	Yes	No	Primary Responsibility	Target Date for Completion

Decision-Making Indicators

B. Data and Research *(continued)*	
Operational Data	
5. The school routinely (at least every 2 years) surveys parents, teachers, and students (middle and high school) to determine perceptions about the school and their connection to it.	
6. The Leadership Team maintains an accessible file of the agendas, minutes, and work products of the Leadership Team, Instructional Teams, and SCC.	
7. The school improvement plan's objectives are linked to action statements with follow-up monitoring of progress.	
Research	
1. The Leadership Team maintains an accessible file of research on topics tied to the school improvement plan.	
2. Teachers report on what they have learned at conferences and submit relevant information for inclusion in the research file.	
3. Representatives from the school visit other schools to see programs of interest, report their findings, and include the report in the research file.	
4. Instructional Teams investigate topics of particular interest and report their findings, including reports filed in the research file.	
5. Teams and individual teachers use the research files to inform their decisions.	

Assessing the		Adding the Missing Pieces		
Yes	No	Primary Responsibility		Target Date for Completion

Chapter 2 References

Blasé, J., & Kirby, P. (1992). The power of praise—a strategy for effective principals. *NASSP Bulletin, 76*(548), 69-77.

Blasé, J., & Kirby, P. C. (2000). *Bringing out the best in teachers: What effective principals do* (2nd ed.). Thousand Oaks, CA: Corwin Press.

Evans, R. (1993, September). The human face of reform. *Educational Leadership, 51*(1), 19-23.

Flanigan, J. L. (1990, August). The principal of the 90's: Changing expectations realized? Paper presented at the Annual Meeting of the National Council of Professors of Educational Administration, Los Angeles, CA. (ERIC Document Reproduction Service No. 342 116)

Fullan, M. (1993). *Change forces: Probing the depths of educational reform.* London: The Falmer Press.

Lambert, L. (2003). *Leadership capacity for lasting school improvement.* Alexandria, VA: Association for Supervision and Curriculum Development.

Lortie, D. C. (1975). *Schoolteacher: A sociological study.* Chicago: University of Chicago Press.

Marzano, R. (2003). *What works in schools: Translating research into action.* Alexandria, VA: Association for Supervision and Curriculum Development.

Rosenholtz, S. (1991). *Teacher's workplace.* New York: Teacher's College Press.

Sashkin, M., & Egermeier, J. (1993). *School change models and processes: A review and synthesis of research and practice.* (ERIC Document Reproduction Service No. 351 757)

Schaffer, R. H. (1988). *The breakthrough strategy: Using short-term successes to build the high-performance organization.* New York: Harper Business.

Schlechty, P. C. (1990). *Schools for the 21st century.* San Francisco: Jossey-Bass.

Schmoker, M. (1996). *Results: The key to continuous school improvement.* Alexandria, VA: Association for Supervision and Curriculum Development.

CHAPTER THREE
Learning—It's A Big World Out There

The mind is a magnificent thing. From the day a baby is born (actually, even before that day), sounds, images, scents, and sensations of touch flood into the brain. The mind makes meaning from it all by sorting impressions into categories and attaching interpretations and emotions to them. One cluster—a smiling face, soothing voice, warm touch—becomes Mommy. The years add a million subtle refinements to that first definition of this one Other. Another cluster—the one with the tummy in the middle that is sometimes full and sometimes aching to be filled, the one with the mouth that spreads into a grin when Mommy is near, the one with the wobbly legs that move it about—becomes Me. Doggy is that curious cluster with the cold nose, soft coat, too many legs, and strange voice. Learning is the process by which the mind makes meaning from a huge world by separating, clustering, and sometimes ignoring the infinite sensations that bombard us from the world and that also arise within us.

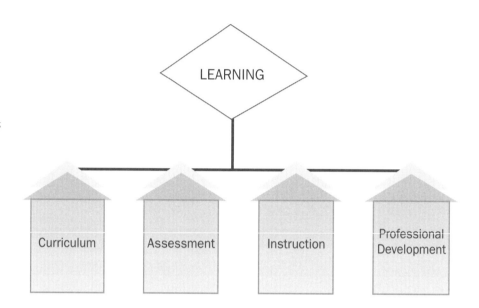

The curriculum is the result of someone deciding what children must understand and must know how to do, and the approximate order in which these things are learned.

The mind also organizes, regulates, notices, and makes meaning out of our actions. The child not only comes to "know" about the world, but also to "act" in the world. The child reaches with a hand, shakes her head to say "no," crawls, walks, speaks words, holds a spoon, pokes the doggy with a stick, runs away when the doggy yips, cries to get Mommy's attention. Before you know it, the child is scribbling with a crayon on the wall, then writing the first letter of her name, and counting the fingers on her hand, touching them one by one.

Because the world is huge and the sensations it evokes infinite, children go to school, where someone gives the child's mind some help by deciding what information can be ignored, what information must be known, how that information is organized, and in what order the child will most successfully acquire it and fit it into her scheme of things. Someone has decided that forming the shapes of letters, drawing arms and legs on the circle that becomes a man, and saying "thank you" are important ways to act. Poking your desk mate with a pencil is not.

The curriculum is the result of someone deciding what children must understand and must know how to do, and the approximate order in which these things are learned. The curriculum also includes larger chunks of knowing and doing that a child may also learn and approaches by which learning is accomplished most efficiently.

Because the mind is a marvelously complex instrument, children are intricately complicated. The curriculum might remain bound in a set of volumes, arranged in neat order on a long shelf, except for … teachers. The teacher is a marvelous and complex invention. The teacher knows the curriculum, and the teacher knows the child and the child's mind. In a miraculous process we call "instruction," the teacher brings together the curriculum and the child's mind. With her own innumerable skills, the teacher makes thousands of decisions to help the child master the curriculum and acquire the capacity and desire to go right on learning beyond the curriculum itself. Through instruction, the child masters the curriculum efficiently.

Making instructional decisions about a child's learning requires the teacher to know the curriculum, know the child's mind, and know the child's progress in mastering the curriculum. The teacher must also know a variety of ways to bring the child and the curriculum together, and which ways are most likely to be effective with which children. The instructional ways are what we call "teaching modes," which are closely associated with the materials teachers provide. "Assessment" is what we call the many methods teachers employ to obtain information about a child's progress in mastering the curriculum so that the teacher can make proper instructional decisions about teaching modes and materials.

All this may sound mechanical, and effective teachers do use organizational systems to efficiently transform curriculum into instructional modes and materials. They also assess students in precise and quantifiable ways to get the most accurate appraisal of their mastery and to make the best decisions about the correct instructional paths. But there is more to teaching than the application of organizational systems. Remember, the child's mind is a marvelous and complex thing, and its dimensions do not always comfortably fit our organizational frameworks. Motivation, the attitude that predisposes a child to pursue a learning task and persist with it, adds a psychological wildcard to the instructional equation that requires of the teacher a deftness of approach as well as a further understanding of the workings of a child's mind.

In this chapter, we will examine how a curriculum is developed and how its mastery is assessed. We will also look at the instructional components of teaching modes, materials, and motivational considerations. In this way, we have chosen to categorize school learning into our own clusters of meaning—curriculum, assessment, instruction, and professional development. That's one way for a mind to organize this little slice of the world—school learning.

MOTIVATION,

the attitude that predisposes a child to pursue a learning task and persist with it, adds a psychological wildcard to the instructional equation that requires of the teacher a deftness of approach as well as a further understanding of the workings of a child's mind.

All the Moving Parts

When you open up a school and look inside, you find a lot of moving parts. If the school is a smoothly functioning system, the parts are moving in synch with one another, each with its own purpose but also contributing to the school's purpose. Clusters of these parts form subsystems within the big system of the school. Think of it as an intricate clock with wheels that spin and turn with specialized precision, some forming a subsystem to mark each advancing second, and others ticking forward on their axes to gather seconds into minutes. Some parts work together to turn the hands and others cooperate to set the pendulum in motion or sound the chime. When every part and every subsystem of parts does its job, the clock's hands will turn and point to the right numbers on the dial. Get a little sand in a gear, and the whole operation goes funky.

In Chapter 2 we looked at subsystems for decision-making. When they are well-oiled and wound to the correct tension, teams meet for sufficient amounts of time, looking at information (data and research) that is timely and appropriate, and making decisions that affect and enhance the performance of other systems in the school.

In Chapter 3, we are examining the subsystem of learning, the mainspring, the heart of the school, the subsystem for which all other subsystems labor. Just as a clock has its own vocabulary of parts— verges and pallets, pendulum bobs and gong wires, chime rods and hands—so also does the Mega System. Before we hold our jeweler's glass to our eye and peer into the moving parts of the subsystem of learning, let's label some of the parts that have a special meaning in the Mega System.

Curriculum Terms

Bloom's Taxonomy – a method for leveling student objectives that allows teachers to create learning strategies which address different cognitive skill levels. The levels in ascending order of difficulty are: knowledge, comprehension, application, analysis, synthesis, and evaluation.

All the Moving Parts

Enhanced Objective—an objective that is related to the target objective but of a higher order, possibly from a higher grade level, but approachable by students who have shown mastery of the target objective.

Learning Plan Grid—a structure for a team of teachers to organize activities that are aligned to curricular objectives. The grid provides areas to identify differentiated activities (teacher/co-teacher centers, activity center, cooperative center, independent work, homework), and by levels of objectives (*prerequisite, target, enhanced*).

Prerequisite Objective—an objective level below that of the *target* (typically grade level) *objective*, but one that is a building block to the *target objective*.

Target Objective—an objective appropriate for most students in the class, typically an objective that is "on grade level."

Unit of Instruction—typically a three to six week block of instruction within a subject area, with objectives organized within a theme.

Unit Plan—a plan developed by the *Instructional Team* to define a *unit of instruction* and outline the standards and objectives addressed in the *unit of instruction*.

Assessment Terms

Class Progress Chart—a record of objectives for the *unit of instruction* and a running account of which students have met each objective.

Unit Test—a test or other assessment device, aligned with each objective covered in the unit, that is developed by the *Instructional Team* for each *unit of instruction* and is administered to all students served by that team before and after the *unit of instruction*.

Instruction Terms

Co-Teachers—teachers such as special education teachers and reading specialists, who assist the classroom teacher by working with individual students and small groups of students during *work time* and their activities are coordinated by the classroom teacher, who shares with them information about student progress.

Learning Centers (or Work Stations)—designated areas in the classroom where students can practice, remediate or enrich objective-based skills, facts, and concepts. *Learning centers* allow teachers to interact with students and provide feedback, while students learn to operate with self-direction. Standard *learning centers* in the classroom are:

- *Teacher center*, where the teacher works with individual students or small groups of students;
- *Co-teacher center*, where a co-teacher such as a special education teacher or reading specialist works with an individual student or group of students during work time;
- *Cooperative center*, where students share a common learning objective, engage in cooperative learning activities, and arrive at a common end product;
- *Activity center*, where each student completes activities individually, or peer-to-peer; and
- *Exploratory center*, a center with a range of high-interest activities related to objectives but selected by the student; the classroom library is located near the *exploratory center*.

Student Learning Plan—typically a one-week or two-week plan developed by the teacher for a student focused on that student's assessed prior learning and next appropriate objectives. Activities on the plan are selected from the *learning plan grids* developed by the *Instructional Team*. One SLP is developed for each subject area.

Targeted Learning—the teacher plans instruction to address each student's assessed prior learning, while students participate in the management of their plan, thereby becoming more responsible for what and how they learn. The *target* is where the student, teacher, and curricular objectives meet and learning takes place.

All the Moving Parts

Whole-Class Instruction—that part of instructional time during which the teacher is presenting new material, reviewing, questioning, and drilling with the entire class. The teacher works from the *teacher center*, moving about the room to achieve eye contact with each student.

Work Time—that part of instructional time during which each student follows his or her *Student Learning Plan*. The purposes of *work time* are to: 1) practice and master concepts and skills, 2) encourage self-directed learning, 3) individualize learning activities, 4) make best use of time, and 5) allow the teacher flexibility to work with individual students or small groups of students.

Curriculum: What Students Must Know and Do

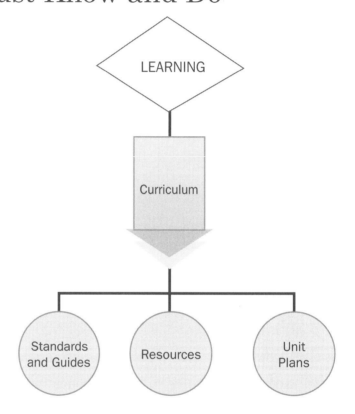

The school's curriculum is what the school intends for students to learn. Of course, children learn a lot of things that are not included in the school's curriculum. Before they step foot in a school, the wiring in children's brains and the rapid cognitive integration in the early years prod children to learn by imitating, by experimenting, and by stubborn mastery of the next predictable skill. They wave bye-bye, scoot and crawl, walk, learn the meaning of words. They learn incidentally, informally, by virtue of living. Curiosity, a desire to please their parents, and the satisfaction of mastery drive early learning. These motivators are no less important in school learning, but the school's curriculum is of a different nature than either the infant and toddler's maturation-driven acquisition of predictable skills or the pre-schooler's random and incidental accumulation of information from the world around him. School learning is efficient learning, taking the child beyond the universal, cognitively-mapped sequence of psychomotor development, beyond the random absorption and integration of words, associations, and understandings.

Curriculum: What Students Must Know and Do

School learning is efficient because of the curriculum. Out of the infinite universe of "things to know and do," the school carves meaningful chunks, organizes them, sequences them, and makes them accessible to students. While the school may intentionally teach its students to master a set of skills and body of knowledge that the school calls its curriculum, a good school also provides opportunity, encouragement, and strategies by which the students acquire skills and knowledge ranging far beyond the stated curriculum. Teachers develop a taught and learned curriculum based on standards with open doors to wider learning. The school also teaches the child efficient ways to explore, organize, and understand what lies beyond its curriculum. The school teaches the child to learn intentionally and efficiently.

School learning is efficient because of the curriculum. Out of the infinite universe of "things to know and do," the school carves meaningful chunks, organizes them, sequences them, and makes them accessible to students.

In an effective system, teachers, working in teams, build curriculum from learning standards, curriculum guides, and a variety of resources, including textbooks, other commercial materials, and teacher-created activities and materials. Teachers organize the curriculum into unit plans that guide instruction for all students and for each student. The unit plans assure that students master standards-based objectives and also provide opportunities for enhanced learning.

Standards and Guides

We now live in a world of learning standards. Standards and benchmarks help us gauge the pace of student mastery of the curriculum; they establish a structure of "floors," levels of mastery to be met and exceeded at points in time. Standards were first created by associations of teachers and educationists with special interest and expertise in particular subject areas such as reading, mathematics, social studies, and science. Then, mostly during the 1990s, states took the standards created by the associations into consideration and designed their own standards. Typically, state departments of education collaborated with subject area associations and teachers in their states to develop learning standards. A common arrangement was to first organize the huge world into domains such as English/Language Arts, Mathematics, Social Studies, Science, Fine Arts, and Physical Education. Recently, Illinois added Social/Emotional Learning as a domain. Other states may follow suit. Within each domain, the standards-writers established a few goals, usually not more than four or five goals per domain. Under English/Language

Arts might be found goals like "Read with understanding and fluency" and "Write to communicate for a variety of purposes." Under Mathematics a goal would be to "Demonstrate and apply a knowledge and sense of numbers, including numeration and operations (addition, subtraction, multiplication, division), patterns, ratios, and proportions" or "Use geometric methods to analyze, categorize, and draw conclusions about points, lines, planes, and space." Goals are the ultimate expectation for the student at the end of the schooling trail.

Because a goal is global, it is also general. For sake of specificity, standards are developed to further define what is subsumed within the goal. For each goal, three or four standards will usually do. A standard associated with the goal of "reading with understanding and fluency" would be to "apply word analysis and vocabulary skills to comprehend selections." A standard for the mathematics goal for "use of geometric methods" would be to "identify, describe, classify, and compare relationships using points, lines, planes, and space." If goals are global and general, standards are one step toward specificity, but a third-grade teacher would hardly know where to begin in preparing a student to someday apply geometric methods without a little more guidance.

Standards had to be made relevant to the grade level. That is not quite as simple as it sounds. When you consider all the students in a third-grade classroom, let alone all the third-graders in a state, the range of what might reasonably be expected is fairly wide. Standards cannot be so precise as to create a "ceiling" for student learning instead of a "floor." So standards-writers in each state invented "benchmarks," which are something like "objectives," but not quite so specific yet. The benchmarks are often provided for a group of grade levels (primary or intermediate, for example) rather than a specific grade level, to give some latitude for teachers as they plot the course of their students' mastery en route to the standard and the ultimate goal.

State learning standards provide a floor, a minimum but necessary set of knowledge and skills that all students should master. Standards, and their related benchmarks and grade-level expectations, give a curriculum a skeleton. Commonly, districts have aligned their curriculum guides to state standards and benchmarks. Textbooks are now aligned to standards. The gap that persists is between the aligned curriculum guide and the learning tasks provided each student.

Curriculum: What Students Must Know and Do

Alignment is a process of matching up the written curriculum (the one that appears in curriculum guides for a school or district) with the tested curriculum (the one that appears in the tests) and the supported curriculum (the one that appears in textbooks and other resources) to make the taught curriculum (the one the teacher actually delivers) more effective. The alignment process serves two related purposes: It serves as a check on guide/text/test congruence, and it provides teachers with an organizational structure for their own planning (Glatthorn, 1995).

Even with the common set of learning objectives that is provided by state learning standards and assessments, a haphazardness in the classroom remains, created in part by the bewildering array of options teachers have for teaching. "Teachers pick and choose from among these options to teach an increasingly idiosyncratic versus common set of learning objectives and skills—even though common standards are essential to clear communication, coherence, and alignment among instructional effort, resources, and programs" (Rosenholtz, 1991, pp. 17-18). State standards and assessments, then, are one step toward solving the problem of "haphazardness." The next big step is for teachers to align their "taught curriculum" with standards. Finally, the taught curriculum is aligned, not for the class as a whole, but for each individual student.

The curriculum, materials, and learning activities are organized so that the teacher can target instruction to each student's level of mastery.

Resources

Teachers construct the taught curriculum from a handful of sources—the state standards and benchmarks, the district curriculum guide, the school's curriculum syllabus, textbooks, other commercial material, and materials developed by the teachers. The teachers organize all of these sources of information into lesson plans that guide their instruction. The Mega System provides teachers with an orderly method for constructing their daily, weekly, and unit lesson plans, aligned to standards-based objectives. The curriculum, materials, and learning activities are organized so that the teacher can target instruction to each student's level of mastery. The system works with instructional units, usually three to six weeks in duration, developed by the Instructional Team for each subject. The unit plan also includes pre-tests and post-tests—quick assessments aligned to standards-based objectives that guide the teacher in individualizing instruction through Student Learning Plans. The system takes full advantage of the learning activities and materials developed by teachers and teams of teachers. The heart of the Mega System's instructional planning is described in detail in the next few sections.

Curriculum: What
Students Must Know and Do

Unit Plans

A unit of instruction is typically three to six weeks of work within a subject area. In the Mega System, an Instructional Team develops a plan for each unit, and the plan is shared by all the teachers who teach that subject and grade level. The unit plan defines the topic or theme of the unit of instruction and then carefully aligns the following:

- State Standards and Benchmarks
- District Curriculum Guidelines
- School Curriculum Guidelines
- Standards/Benchmark-Based Objectives
- Criteria for Mastery
- Unit Pre-Test and Post-Test Items
- Leveled and Differentiated Learning Activities

A unit test is an assessment device, aligned with each objective covered in the unit, and administered to all students before and after the unit of instruction (or smaller parts of the unit). The pre-test and post-test are the same test, or parallel items for the same objectives, given at the beginning and end of a unit. In some cases, especially in the lower grades, the unit test is divided into a series of smaller tests, given before and after instruction in the objectives covered on the smaller test. Unit tests are constructed to give teachers a good idea of a student's current level of mastery of the objectives without taking a great amount of time to administer. A unit test need not be a pencil and paper test, especially in the lower grades, but is a way for the teacher to specifically check each student's mastery of each objective in a manner that is not time consuming.

The Unit Plan forms on the following page show how target objectives are aligned to grade-level or grade-cluster benchmarks, criteria for mastery, and items for the pre-/post-test.

Unit Plan Example

Page: 1

Grade Level: 3rd   Subject: Reading   Unit of Instruction Code: 3R01

Unit of Instruction Title: Effective Communication

Standard/ Benchmark (Code)	Target Objectives (with Objective Code Prefix)	Objective Descriptor	Criteria for Mastery	Pre-Test/ Post Test Items
A3	3R01-01T Construct proper sentences using correct grammar, punctuation, capitalization.	Sentence structure	When given a rubric that provides proper sentence structure, the student develops properly written sentences with 80% mastery.	1. Given a bank of vocabulary words, the student writes two proper sentences.
A3	3R01-02T Determine the appropriate use of imperative and exclamatory sentences.	Oral reading	The student marks the correct punctuation for imperative and exclamatory sentences with 80% mastery.	2. Given a variety of unmarked sentences, the student correctly marks and identifies sentence.

Unit Plan

Page: _____

Grade Level: _____ Subject: _____ Unit of Instruction Code: _____

Unit of Instruction Title: _____

Standard/ Benchmark (Code)	Target Objectives (with Objective Code Prefix)	Objective Descriptor	Criteria for Mastery	Pre-Test/ Post Test Items

*Curriculum: What
Students Must Know and Do*

Leveled and Differentiated Learning Activities

Learning activities, the assignments given to each student targeted to that student's level of mastery, are carefully aligned with the objectives included in the unit plan to provide a variety of ways for a student to achieve mastery as evidenced in *both* the successful completion of the learning activities and correct responses on the unit post-test.

The learning plan grid provides a structure for a team of teachers to organize learning activities that are aligned to one curricular objective in the unit plan. The grid provides areas to identify differentiated activities (teacher/co-teacher centers, activity center, cooperative center, independent work, homework), and levels of objectives (prerequisite, target, enhanced).

An activity instructions form is created for each activity on the learning plan grid. For centers (or work stations), a copy of the activity instructions form may be laminated and placed at the center with the necessary materials.

The Learning Plan Grid forms on the following page show how a target objective is leveled to produce prerequisite and enhanced objectives and how each objective is aligned with learning activities in various settings.

Learning Plan Grid (Example)

Standard/Benchmark Code: <u>A3</u>

Target Objective Code: <u>3R01-01T</u>   Enhanced Objective Code: <u>3R01-01E</u>   Prerequisite code: <u>3R01-01P</u>

Objective	Independent	Activity Center	Cooperative Center	Teacher Center/ Co-Teacher Center	Homework
Enhanced: *Construct in coherent narrative form a series of related sentences.*	*Enrichment p. 24, A & B*	1. Develop a written conversation between two people (friends, parents, others) using declarative and interrogative sentences.		*Discuss the inflections of speech in declarative & interrogative sentence usage*	*p. 28, 19-25, Add words to complete sentence*
Target: *Construct proper sentences using correct grammar, punctuation, capitalization.*	*Practice p. 20, C & D*	2. Use proper sentence structure with activity	*Create a short skit (3-5 minutes) on the computer using proper sentence structure, include int. and dec. sentences. Share oral and written work with class.*	*On-the-spot slate writing: look for correct punctuation, capitalization, etc.*	*p. 3, 16-20*
Prerequisite: *Assemble correct sentences when given words using manipulatives.*	*Review p. 17, 1-15*	3. Build sentences with word tiles.		*Write on chart paper student oral created sentences, discussing and highlighting, punctuation, capitalization, etc.*	*p. 3, 6-15, Label a sentence or not a sentence*

Exploratory Topics: Feature "Great Valley Train" as library selection. Use vocabulary discovery box.

Learning Plan Grid

Standard/Benchmark Code: _____

Target Objective Code: _____   Enhanced Objective Code: _____   Prerequisite code: _____

Objective	Independent	Activity Center	Cooperative Center	Teacher Center/ Co-Teacher Center	Homework
Enhanced					
Target					
Prerequisite					

Exploratory topics:

Collaborative Development of the Unit Plan

The unit plan is developed by the Instructional Team in the Mega System to define a unit of instruction and outline the standards/benchmarks and target objectives (typically grade level) addressed in the unit of instruction. A unit of instruction is typically three to six weeks of work within a subject area. The Instructional Team:

1. Determines the concepts, principles, and skills that will be covered within the unit.
2. Identifies the standards/benchmarks that apply to the grade level and unit topic.
3. Develops all objectives that clearly align to the selected standards/benchmarks.
4. Arranges the objectives in sequential order.
5. Determines the best objective descriptors.
6. Considers the most appropriate elements for mastery and constructs criteria for mastery.
7. Develops pre/post test items that are clear and specific and would provide evidence of mastery consistent with the criteria established.

The unit plan aligns the curriculum to standards and benchmarks. The next step is to align the curriculum to instruction. This is where the real fun begins—teachers sharing their most successful instructional strategies for meeting each objective in the unit of instruction. Learning plan grids level each objective into three tiers—target, enhanced, and prerequisite. The learning plan grid also differentiates learning activities among various settings—independent work, activity center, cooperative center, teacher center, co-teacher center, and homework. The learning plan grid records ideas for the exploratory center. An activity may appear on more than one grid. Once learning plan grids are prepared for all the objectives in the unit of instruction, activity instructions are prepared for each cell on the grid. The activity instructions provide the detail that enables any teacher to use the learning activity, and also become a means of explaining the activity to students.

Curriculum: What Students Must Know and Do

▶ The Instructional Team's Preparation

To begin its work in developing units of instruction, the Instructional Team gathers all resources that support and guide instruction in the classroom:

- state academic standards,
- grade level benchmarks and performance indicators,
- district curriculum,
- scope and sequence of district curriculum,
- expectations of state assessment for relevant grades and subjects,
- district assessments,
- individual classroom lesson plans,
- textbook series resources, and
- other specific grade level/subject resources.

With this information at hand, the Instructional Team begins to knit together units of instruction, integrating curriculum, assessment, and instruction and aligning it all with standards.

▶ Organizing Units and Aligning Benchmarks

In some districts, a curriculum map or scope-and-sequence has already defined unit topics and clustered benchmarks within them. The district curriculum guide may even organize grade-level performance indicators to provide the stepping stones to the benchmarks. Since benchmarks are provided by ranges of grade (such as K-3, 4-5, 6-8, and 9-11), other grades need to "design down"—planning the appropriate steps leading to the benchmark.

Depending upon the degree of specificity provided by the district curriculum, the Instructional Team will adopt or develop unit topics and benchmarks for each grade level and subject. Instructional Teams will then "articulate" the units from grade level to grade level, seeking appropriate sequence and fluency. In middle school and high school, course sequence may be more significant than grade/class level.

When developing unit topics and benchmarks clusters, the Instructional Team reviews ALL of the standards/benchmarks. The team considers the key concepts. The team examines the principles and skills suggested within each standard/benchmark. The team thinks about how the essential ideas can be clustered within a unit of instruction (i.e., How can reading and writing standards work together? or How do computation and problem-solving connect?).

▶ Developing Target Objectives ("The student will be able to...")

Instructional Teams think about what the benchmarks are suggesting as the "target" for that grade level. They consider the verb that defines exactly what students should be able to do (i.e., identify, distinguish, write, use, present, demonstrate) at that grade level. They discuss and define what level of student action is expected toward the benchmark. The Instructional Team develops objectives to reflect the appropriate level of students' action. They discuss how students will show their mastery of that target objective.

A target objective is specific and:

- **aimed at the benchmark** and appropriate to the grade level
- sufficiently **specific** that it can be taught and **mastered within a week**
- specific to one student
- expressed as "The student will be able to..." **SWBAT** (this may be an "assumed" prefix of each objective when writing the objectives)
- expressed as **observable** or **measurable** student action
- descriptive of the student's **performance behavior**— what the student shows he/she knows or can do

Curriculum: What Students Must Know and Do

▶ Criteria for Mastery (Conditions and Level of Accuracy)

The objective itself simply states what the student will be able to do: "The student will be able to identify nouns." The criteria for mastery give the *conditions* under which the objective will be met and the *level of accuracy* that is expected. The pre-test is for quick and convenient diagnostic purposes. The criteria for mastery is harder evidence of mastery, more likely to be exhibited by assignments completed during the week rather than on a pre-test or post-test. The exception to this rule is often found in middle school and high school, where the teacher may give a more thorough pre-test and post-test, serving the purpose of diagnosis as the pre-test and more thorough demonstration of mastery on the post-test.

Consider the target objective, "The student will be able to add a series of 4, single-digit numbers." The criteria for mastery might say: "Given 10 problems to solve, the student will answer 80% correctly." The "given 10 problems to solve" is the *condition* part of the statement. The 80% is the *level of accuracy*. Some objectives lend themselves to a level of accuracy that is less than 100%, and some do not. If the objective is to divide fractions, the teacher may decide that if a student gets 8 out of 10 problems correct, he or she has probably mastered the objective but made a couple calculation errors. However, if the objective is to print the student's first name, the teacher may expect 100% accuracy. "Asked to print name three times, the student spells it correctly and forms letters properly all three times."

Criteria for Mastery often use references to time ("within 10 minutes"), quantity ("list 5 nouns"), accuracy ("to the nearest 100"), and/or quality ("with 3 or fewer punctuation errors").

Pre-Test/Post-Test Items

The pre-test is used as a quick assessment, a way for the teacher to assess each student's readiness for an objective in order for the teacher to make appropriate assignments on the Student Learning Plan. Likewise, the post-test is a way to get a quick read on students' mastery after completion of the unit or after completion of the period of instruction allotted for the objective. The pre-test and the post-test are the same—a before and an after, or parallel items of the same level of difficulty. In other words, the post-test isn't "harder" than the pre-test. The "items" need not be pencil and paper test items. The teacher may give the pre-test for a unit all at one time or in chunks, prior to addressing each new set of objectives. If the items are taken from a chapter test or other material, the Instructional Team indicates the specific items that correspond with the objective. The chapter test may include more items than the pre-test/post-test, of course. Pre-tests should not be graded. Post-tests may be graded, or included as part of larger graded tests. Between the pre-test and the post-test, students complete a variety of learning activities, including independent work and homework. They may also take other graded tests. Teachers have several ways to determine mastery through the instructional process. The pre-test and post-test address only target objectives. The teacher assesses for mastery of prerequisite and enhanced objectives through learning activities.

When writing pre-test/post-test items, it is important to note the level of the objective within Bloom's Taxonomy: Knowledge, Comprehension, Application, Analysis, Synthesis, or Evaluation. The test items should match the taxonomy level of the objective.

Prerequisite Objectives

Sometimes the pre-test and/or subsequent work by the student demonstrates that the student is not ready to tackle the target objective. The teacher's goal is always to get every student to mastery of the target objective by the end of the unit, but students do not start in the same place. Bloom's Verbs are one way to "level" an objective by establishing a prerequisite step to the target objective. Another way is to look at the target objective for the next lower grade level (or course sequence) and adjust it up a little closer to the target objective. The prerequisite objective is a building block to the target objective.

Curriculum: What Students Must Know and Do

▶ Enhanced Objectives

Some students demonstrate early mastery of an objective and are bored if kept with the rest of the class. The enhanced objective is based on the target objective but is more demanding of the student. Bloom's Verbs are one way to "level" an objective by establishing an enhanced step above the target objective. Another way is to look at the target objective for the next higher grade level (or course sequence) and adjust it down a little closer to the target objective.

▶ Examples of Objectives

Target Objective: The student will be able to name the four primary directions on a navigational compass. (This is an objective at the level of general knowledge.)

Criteria for mastery: Given a blank compass face, the student will write the name of the four primary directions in the correct locations.

Pre-test/Post-test item: Mark the four primary directions on the blank compass face.

Prerequisite Objective: The student will be able to identify the four primary directions on a navigational compass by matching the points to a list of North, South, East, West. (This is an objective at the level of general knowledge.)

Enhanced Objective: The student will be able to write a short paragraph explaining the positions of the four primary directions on a navigational compass. (This is an objective at the comprehension level.)

Assessment: Knowing What Each Student Knows and Can Do

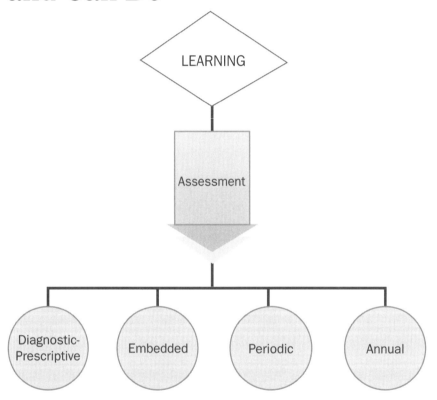

Assessment is the process of testing (written, verbal, or by examination of work) to see: 1) what a student knows and can do, and 2) patterns of strength and weakness in what a group of students knows and can do. The value of an assessment is determined by what happens as a consequence of it. The National Academy of Science (1996) explains the evolution of assessment, as it has come to take a more prominent role in school improvement:

> Ideas about assessments have undergone important changes in recent years. In the new view, assessment and learning are two sides of the same coin. Assessments provide an operational definition of standards in that they define in measurable terms what teachers should teach and students should learn. When students engage in assessments, they should learn from those assessments. (pp. 15-16)

Assessment: Knowing What
Each Student Knows and Can Do

It should be noted that teachers assess students informally in ways that we will not discuss here, but that are made obvious later when we discuss instruction. This informal assessment includes the teacher's scanning of the classroom during whole-class instruction, reading the faces of each child, questioning, and then changing course to re-teach or reiterate. The same skillful assessment occurs when teachers interact individually with students, taking the pulse of understanding, knowing what each child knows.

The Mega System helps teachers make practical use of four more formal types of assessment: diagnostic-prescriptive, embedded, periodic, and annual.

Diagnostic-Prescriptive Assessments

Diagnostic/prescriptive assessments are quick, diagnostic tests used to "prescribe" appropriate learning activities for a student or group of students to help them meet objectives. The Mega System includes unit pre-tests and post-tests for this purpose. The test may be a pencil and paper test, oral quizzes, or "show me" assessments that a teacher can quickly and conveniently administer to determine each student's level of mastery of the unit's objectives. The unit tests are created by the Instructional Teams.

Embedded Assessments

Embedded assessments are learning activities aligned to objectives with criteria for mastery which enable a teacher to check mastery within the context of instruction. By completing these assigned activities, the student demonstrates a level of mastery of the objectives the activities are designed to teach or to reinforce. The embedded assessments also serve the purpose of diagnosis, so that the teacher can modify the Student Learning Plan through the course of a unit of instruction.

Assessment: Knowing What
Each Student Knows and Can Do

Periodic Assessments

Periodic assessments, administered for each grade level two to four times a year, enable the teachers and teams to see how students are progressing toward mastery of standards that will be included on state assessments. Periodic assessments may be teacher-made, part of a published curriculum, or created by psychometricians at testing firms. The periodic assessments help teachers modify their diagnostic/prescriptive assessments and their learning activities to bring a closer alignment between instruction and the annual standards-based assessments.

Annual Assessments

State standards assessments (criterion-referenced) and norm-referenced achievement tests provide an annual appraisal of each student's progress and the school's progress by grade levels and subject area. The timing and nature of these tests make them most useful to the Leadership Team in making program and placement decisions. The Instructional Teams use the annual assessments to improve their unit pre- and post-tests and their learning activities to address areas of general weakness on the annual assessment. Using the same achievement test in basic subject areas for all students in the school is important so that each student's year-to-year progress (value added) can be measured.

Instruction: Teacher and Student

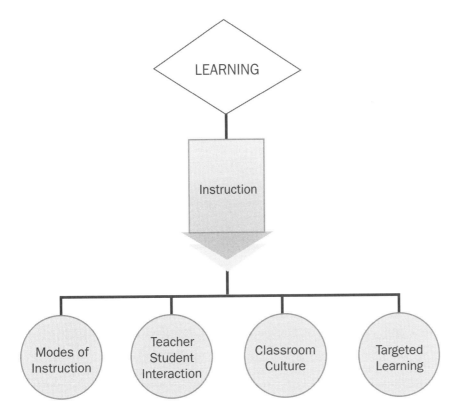

School learning begins with a well-organized curriculum, including teacher presentations and student activities aligned to standards-based objectives. Assessment enables the teacher to know what each student knows and alter the instructional path accordingly. With this careful preparation by teams of teachers, the individual teacher now takes the curriculum to the student through a variety of instructional modes, with the artistry of both social and academic interactions with the student, in a classroom culture supportive of individual mastery. The most widely replicated findings concerning the characteristics of teachers who elicit strong achievement score gains are:

- **Teacher Expectation/Role Definition/Sense of Efficacy:** Teachers accept responsibility for teaching their students. They believe that students are capable of learning. They re-teach if necessary and alter materials as needed.
- **Student Opportunity to Learn:** Teachers allocate most of their available time to instruction, not non-academic activities, and learning activities are carefully aligned to standards.

- **Classroom Management and Organization:** Teachers organize their learning environments and use group management approaches effectively to maximize time students spend engaged in lessons.
- **Curriculum Pacing:** Teachers move through the curriculum rapidly but in small steps that minimize student frustration and allow continuous progress.
- **Active Teaching (sometimes called Direct Instruction):** Teachers actively instruct, demonstrating skills, explaining concepts, conducting participatory activities, reviewing when necessary. They teach their students rather than expecting them to learn mostly from curriculum materials. They do not just stress facts or skills, they also emphasize concepts and understanding.
- **Teaching to Mastery:** Following active instruction, teachers provide opportunities for students to practice and apply learning. They monitor each student's progress and provide feedback and remedial instruction as needed, making sure students achieve mastery.
- **A Supportive Learning Environment:** In addition to their strong academic focus, these teachers maintain pleasant, friendly classrooms and are perceived as enthusiastic, supportive instructors.

(Brophy & Good, 1986; Good, 1996; Reynolds, 1992; Waxman & Walberg, 1991)

The Mega System defines the best practices within a variety of instructional modes and encourages teachers to select the mode appropriate to the student and the task. The Mega System also attends to the motivational factors in learning—the student's desire to learn and persistence in learning.

Mastery Learning and Student Support

The instructional subsystem described in this handbook includes the principles of mastery learning that require close attention to each child's demonstrated mastery of teacher-defined objectives. A basic premise of mastery learning is that nearly all students are capable of mastering objectives targeted to grade-level expectations aligned to benchmarks and standards. Individual students, however, require different instructional approaches and different amounts of time to achieve mastery.

Instruction: Teacher and Student

The Mega System's instructional subsystem carries forth the curricular leveling of objectives, with target objectives directed at the grade-level expectations, prerequisite objectives provided as building-blocks for students not ready for the target objective, and enhanced objectives for students demonstrating early mastery. Likewise, the Mega System, in its suggested process for curriculum development, encourages teams of teachers to plan a variety of learning activities for each level of objective. Instructionally, the teacher uses whole-class instruction, small-group instruction, independent work, homework, and computer-assisted instruction as means for further variation in mode of instructional delivery to account for student differences. Thus, the teacher's quiver is full of planned and prepared activities and materials to individualize instruction according to individual student differences in prior learning.

Even with these multiple methods for accounting for student differences, some students will lag behind. It is a tenet of mastery learning that time is the final variable to adjust to account for student differences in learning. Leveled objectives and learning tasks allow the teacher some fluidity in moving students forward at an individual pace. But again, this will not provide sufficient variation for all students. For lagging students, more instructional time is necessary, and this must be provided beyond regular class time. After-school and tutoring programs directly tied to classroom objectives are one way to provide more time for learning. Homework is another.

The Mega System's instructional methodology accounts for wide diversity of student learning and is effective even with most special education students included in the classroom. For a small group of students, maybe 1% or 2% of all students, variations in instructional methodology and time will not be sufficient to assure mastery of grade-level expectations. For these students, the same instructional methodology will be effective, but the objectives must be realistically adjusted. Special education staff, working with the Instructional Teams, will make these adaptations through their Individual Education Plans. A school may also find it useful to form a Support Team to examine periodic assessment data and devise interventions to support students who are not responding to the regular or special education programs. For some students, counseling, family support, summer programs, and other interventions beyond instructional interventions are necessary.

> It is a tenet of mastery learning that time is the final variable to adjust to account for student differences in learning.

Modes of Instruction

The traditional approach to schooling calls for whole class lessons followed by independent seatwork and homework for practice. Small-group learning, especially in the primary grades, is a popular variation to this approach. Small-group learning may follow the same principles as teacher-directed, whole-class instruction, where the teacher works with a group of students while other students are engaged in other activities. In another form of small-group learning, the students direct the activities, with instructions provided by the teacher. This student-directed, small-group learning allows for active learning with differentiated activities at various centers in the classroom at the same time. Student-directed, small-group learning is an ideal mode for cooperative learning strategies. Other modes of teaching are peer learning and computer-based learning. Research gives us guidance for the most effective practices within each mode of instruction.

> Research gives us guidance for the most effective practices within each mode of instruction.

In order to apply the most exact research evidence to the particular method of teaching, we break teaching/learning into categories. First, we distinguish between teacher-directed instruction and student-directed learning. Both, of course, are teacher planned. Teacher-directed instruction is otherwise known as direct instruction and occurs in a whole-class setting or in a teacher-directed small group. The third variation would be one-on-one, teacher-directed tutoring of an individual student. Student-directed learning may simply be independent work, or seatwork, the completion of assignments by individual students. Student-directed learning may also be in a small-group setting, including cooperative learning methods. Homework, which is student-directed but takes place at home rather than at school, receives its own category.

Teacher-Directed Instruction

An analysis of Quality of Instruction (Walberg, 1984; Wang, Haertel, & Walberg, 1993) finds evidence of the particular strength of the following approaches: instructional elements (cues, reinforcement, corrective feedback, engagement); mastery learning; computer-assisted instruction; comprehension teaching and direct instruction; graded homework with comments; explanatory graphics; adaptive speed-reading training; phonemic awareness; inquiry in writing; and acceleration of gifted students. Mastery learning methods require that students display mastery of one unit of instruction before moving on to the next; time becomes an important factor, as students require different amounts of time to master an objective. Direct instruction

Instruction: Teacher and Student

is teacher-directed instruction (whole-class or small-group) done well, including these phases: 1) review, homework check, and re-teaching if necessary; 2) rapid presentation of new content and skills in small steps; 3) guided student practice with close monitoring by the teacher; 4) corrective feedback and reinforcement; 5) independent practice in seat-time and homework with 90 percent success rates; 6) weekly and monthly reviews. Comprehension teaching is similar to direct instruction and consists of three phases: 1) modeling by the teacher, 2) guided practice—students perform with help from the teacher, and 3) application—students perform independently.

Particular techniques employed during teacher-directed instruction have demonstrated impressive power (effect sizes) in studies of student learning. Cues, for example, are especially effective in activating prior knowledge and alerting students to important information (Walberg & Lai, 1999). Connecting to prior knowledge is not only helpful in organizing new learning, but increases students' interest in the topic (Alexander, Kulikowich, & Schulze, 1994). Advance organizers, first popularized by psychologist David Ausubel (1968), provide scaffolding for the incorporation of new material to be introduced within the next 20 minutes or so. Advance organizers take such forms as visual graphics, lists, and statements abstracting the material. Simply describing the new content (expository advance organizer) is the most effective type of advance organizer, but other forms (narrative—brief presentation in story form, skimming—quick preview of text, and illustrated—use of visuals) are also effective (Stone, 1983). Internal summaries and the rule-example-rule approach have demonstrated their power in enhancing learning (Rosenshine, 1968). The agile teacher who is able to articulate clear goals and expectations for the lesson and make wise decisions in use of various instructional techniques is key to teacher-directed instruction (Good & Brophy, 2000).

Teacher-Directed Instruction (Whole Class)

The teacher plans whole class instruction at key points within the unit of instruction, typically devoting at least some time each day to whole-class instruction in each subject. The amount of time devoted to whole class instruction versus work time will vary from day to day. The teacher prepares a whole class instruction plan for each whole class instruction period. The plan includes notes to guide the teacher through: Review, Presentation, and Summary.

▶ Review (20% of period)

The teacher begins a whole-class instructional segment by setting the climate for attentive learning, cueing the students to focus in, reinforcing attentive behaviors, reminding students to have their necessary materials at hand, checking postures and facial expressions, and generally encouraging pro-social behavior. This is called a "behavior check." Next the teacher quickly reviews the previous lesson, including homework assignments from it. The teacher uses rapid-fire questioning to review the previous lesson and build a bridge from it to the new lesson. The teacher notes the students' progress in mastering new learning and encourages their self-praise. The teacher checks for areas that need re-teaching.

▶ Presentation (60% of period)

The presentation stage includes three phases: 1) The teacher introduces the new lesson, connecting it to the previous one and to prior learning; 2) The teacher develops interest in the new topic; and 3) The teacher directly teaches the new lesson. In introducing the new lesson, the teacher clearly delineates what the students will learn and what will be expected of them. In creating an interest in the topic, the teacher uses an interest stimulator (illustration, demonstration, model, anecdote), cues, advance organizers, and question sprinkling. In directly teaching the lesson, the teacher, with clarity and enthusiasm, proceeds in small steps, uses both verbal explanations and physical demonstrations, elicits student responses regularly but briefly, and "thinks out loud" throughout, verbalizing the thinking processes. In lengthy presentations, the teacher uses internal summaries at key points.

▶ Summary/Confirmation of Mastery (20% of period)

The teacher chooses appropriate questioning strategies, drilling, recitation, and summative discussion or inquiry to ascertain what the students have learned and to help them rehearse it. The teacher balances the factual recall questions with the higher order thinking questions to evaluate the extent and quality of the student learning during this session. The teacher asks students to put new learning into their own words, to apply what they have learned to solve a problem, and/or to recite memorized facts or passages. The teacher equitably distributes questions among students. The teacher gives quick feedback to student responses. This phase should end with a definite closure statement to assist students in organizing the learning once again.

Instruction: Teacher and Student

The Whole-Class Instruction Plan shown on the next page helps the teacher organize and outline the key components of whole class instruction and tie them to the standards-based objectives addressed during the week. Combined with individual learning activities, developed on the learning plan grids and assigned with Student Learning Plans (described later), the Whole-Class Instruction Plan is the teacher's basic preparation for each week's instruction. Together, the Whole-Class Instruction Plan and Student Learning Plan provide targeted learning in a variety of instructional modes.

Whole-Class Instruction Plan

Week of: _____ Teacher: _____ Subject: _____

Target Objective Code(s): _____

	Monday	Tuesday	Wednesday	Thursday	Friday
Central Purpose of Lesson					
Behavior Check					
Review					
Think					
Know					
Show					

Instruction: Teacher and Student

Whole-Class Instruction Guidelines

The teacher plans whole class instruction at key points within the unit of instruction, typically devoting at least some time each day to whole-class instruction in each subject. The amount of time devoted to whole class instruction versus work time will vary from day to day. The teacher prepares a whole class instruction plan for each whole class instruction segment. The plan includes notes to guide the teacher through: Behavior Check, Review and Homework Check, Think, Know, and Show.

Behavior Check

Time: Approximately 1 to 2 minutes

Purpose: To set the psychological climate in the classroom; cue students to focus in; reinforce attentive behaviors

Method: Teacher in his/her station, students have learning materials on desks and in order, students in learning posture, smiles on faces. Pro-social behavioral expectations reinforced by teacher.

Review (and Homework Check)

Time: 5 to 8 minutes

Purposes: To provide students with clear evaluations of their progress in attaining learning goals (Marzano, 2003); To detect areas that need further teaching or practice; To connect prior learning with new learning

Method: May include homework check. To review: Teacher asks fairly rapid-fire questions from previous lesson to build a bridge to today's new learning. Teacher calls on students in rotation, using various methods. Teacher sprinkles in verbal reinforcement about the progress and understanding students are demonstrating. This is followed with a "rope" (anything to lasso or draw in the students' attention).The "rope" signals the transition to the *Think* segment, where the new lesson is introduced.

Think

Time: Approximately 20% of the *Think/Know/Show* sequence time

Purpose: To introduce new lesson; continue activating prior knowledge; stimulate student cognition relative to the topic

Methods: Cues, Advance Organizers, Sprinkling of Questions

- **Cues** are one of the top 4 selected teacher effectiveness strategies in the Walberg research (Walberg, 1999). Cueing students on what is to be learned and how to learn it activates prior knowledge; students look for what they expect to see as the lesson unfolds, based on where teacher has told them to focus.
  - Cues involve "hints" about what students are about to experience.
  - Cues should focus on what is important as opposed to what is unusual.
  - Research indicates that the more students know about a topic, the more they tend to be interested in it (Alexander, Kulikowich, & Schulze, 1994).
- **Questions** are effective learning tools even when asked *before* a learning experience, so sprinkle them in as part of the learning "set."
- **Advance Organizers** were first popularized by psychologist David Ausubel (1968) who defined them as: "appropriately relevant and inclusive introductory materials…introduced in advance of learning…and presented at a higher level of abstraction, generality, and inclusiveness than the information presented after it. The organizer serves to provide ideational scaffolding for the stable incorporation and retention of the more detailed and differentiated materials that follow. Thus, advance organizers are not the same as summaries or overviews….but rather are designed to bridge the gap between what the learner already knows and what he needs to know before he can successfully learn the task at hand" (p. 148).

Instruction: Teacher and Student

An **Advance Organizer** can be:

- A graphic, a visual
- A list
- A statement
- Anything that helps students focus on the main idea
- Anything that helps students order their thoughts
- Anything that helps students relate to material that might otherwise seem fragmented
- Anything that helps students know what they're expected to learn in the next 20 minutes and why it is important

Advance Organizers can produce different results:

- Four general types: expository, narrative, skimming, illustrated
- All produce fairly powerful results, but **expository** has the largest effect size (Stone, 1983).

  Expository: simply describe the new content to which students are going to be exposed

  Narrative: present information to students in a story format

  Skimming: used with text that is going to be presented. Teacher asks students to skim, or briefly look at, certain pages, pictures, etc.

  Illustrated: non-linguistic, visual representation of the material to be covered; a graphic organizer is another term for this. Usually shows the main topic in the center, with subtopics on "arms"

Summing Up *Think*: The *Think* segment of *whole-class instruction* is signaled by a "rope"—an interest stimulator—to focus student attention on the introduction of the new lesson for the day. The teacher chooses cues, questions, and/or advance organizers to preview the day's lesson in a fast-paced presentation of 5 minutes or so. These strategies assist students in activating their prior knowledge and provide them a framework for organizing what is coming next.

Know

Time: Approximately 60% of the *Think/Know/Show* sequence time

Purpose: To directly teach the new skills or concepts

Methods: Lecture, Demonstration, Modeling

- With clarity and enthusiasm, teacher directly communicates what the students need to know
- Teacher proceeds in small steps
- Teacher uses both verbal explanations and physical demonstrations
- Teacher elicits student responses regularly, occasionally questions (engagement)
- Teacher "thinks out loud" throughout, verbalizing the thinking processes
- If presentation is lengthier, teacher gives internal summaries at key points (Rosenshine, 1968)
- "Rule-example-rule" approach

Summing Up *Know*: There will be a variety of strategies employed during this direct teaching segment. This is where "teacher decision-making, guided by clear goals, is the key to effective instruction" (Good & Brophy, 2000, p. 375).

Show

Time: Approximately 20% of the *Think/Know/Show* sequence time

Purpose: To find out what students have learned and rehearse their learning

Methods: Conducting Verbal Drills, Recitations; Discussions; Quiz Games

Instruction: Teacher and Student

- Teacher asks students to put new learning into their own words
- Teacher asks students to apply what they have just learned in solving a problem
- Teacher may ask class to recite memorized facts or passages
- Teacher utilizes the 6 Characteristics of Good Questions (Grossier, 1964) when conducting recitations. Questions are: Clear, Purposeful, Brief, Natural, Sequenced, Thought Provoking
- Teacher equitably distributes questions among students
- Teacher gives quick feedback about student responses

The End of Show

The end of the *Show* segment includes lesson closure. This is where the "ribbon" comes in. It signifies a wrap up to the learning and prompts students where to store the information for later retrieval.

- Teacher finishes the *Show* segment with a quick review of the lesson's main points
- Teacher may return to the advance organizer, visual, or "rope" object
- This may only take 2 or 3 minutes, but it is necessary to help students know where and how to store the information they just learned; the teacher is organizing it for the students once more
- Teacher analyzes whether or not re-teaching of the day's concept is necessary
- Teacher does a quick introduction to the Work Time activities, if this has not already been previewed earlier in the day

Summing Up *Show*: The teacher again is the decision-maker, choosing appropriate questioning strategies, discussion, or inquiry to ascertain what the students have learned. The teacher is a master at questioning, balancing the factual recall questions with the higher order thinking questions to evaluate the extent and quality of the student learning during this session. The *Show* segment should end with a definite closure statement (a "ribbon" to tie up the package) to assist students in organizing the learning in their brains once again.

Situational grouping is based on short-term grouping of students that enables the teacher to re-teach, review, and enhance to a specific subset of knowledge and skill needs of students who are in the process of mastering material that has already been presented.

Teacher-Directed Instruction (Small Group)

Teacher-directed, small-group instruction is an effective follow-up to the whole-class presentation, enabling the teacher to focus instructional attention on the particular requirements of homogeneous groups of students. The groupings should be fluid, rearranged frequently in response to particular learning needs. Students should not be clustered in other ways—such as seating arrangements—that appear to solidify group membership and "label" members. Because groups are formed to address particular learning needs, they will vary from time to time in number of members and in the time devoted to them (Good & Brophy, 2000).

Mason and Good (1993) tested two small-group models on 1,700 fourth, fifth, and sixth grade students in 81 mathematics classrooms. In one model, which they called the *structural approach*, students were divided into two homogeneous groups (based on prior proficiency in mathematics) before separately receiving whole-class instruction from a teacher. In the second model, called the *situational approach*, all students received the same whole-class instruction and were then provided follow-up instruction in small groups based on their demonstrated need for review or enrichment. The *situational approach* proved most effective.

A word of caution is in order here. The *situational approach* was effective because it allowed the teacher flexibility in grouping and re-grouping students for specific instructional purposes following introduction of the new material. This is different from traditional ability grouping (such as reading groups) where the group membership tends to remain highly stable once groups are formed, creating a *de facto* "tracking" system with negative consequences (Eder & Felmlee, 1984; Haller, 1985; Hallinan & Sorensen, 1985; Rowan & Miracle, 1983; Weinstein, 1976).

Situational grouping is based on short-term grouping of students that enables the teacher to re-teach, review, and enhance to a specific subset of knowledge and skill needs of students who are in the process of mastering material that has already been presented. Groups should be organized and taught in ways that provide low achievers with the extra instruction they need. Teachers can assign more students to high groups and fewer students to low groups, thus arranging for more intensive instruction of low achievers within the group setting. Or, teachers can spend more of their time providing direct instruction and supervision to low groups while high groups spend more time working cooperatively or independently (Anderson & Pigford, 1988).

Instruction: Teacher and Student

Student-Directed Instruction

Student-directed instruction serves several purposes: Students develop personal responsibility for their learning; they hone their learning skills and meta-cognitive skills; they learn from other students in group settings and in peer teaching arrangements; and the teacher is able to target different learning activities to meet the needs of specific students while also being free to assist some students directly. The most common form of student-directed instruction is independent work, when students complete their assignments individually. This does not mean that they are all completing the same assignment. Once again, the teacher is able, through a Student Learning Plan, to differentiate instruction by giving students assignments consistent with their demonstrated prior learning. With peer teaching, or peer learning, the teacher pairs students to help each other. The act of teaching and assisting another student strengthens the learning of the peer teacher. Instructional time is increased and made specific to the student in this arrangement, as opposed to a teacher instructing all students at the same time. The third type of student-directed instruction is found in small groups of students who complete assignments provided by the teacher for the group. This format provides the opportunity for cooperative learning techniques.

Homework and Communication with Parents

Research has long established the strong influence of a student's home environment on that student's success in school. Less clear has been what schools can do to engage parents in their children's learning. We now have significant, new research that shows that schools can improve their students' learning by engaging parents in ways that directly relate to their children's academic progress, maintaining a consistent message of what is expected of parents, and reaching parents directly, personally, and with a trusting approach (Epstein, 1995; Henderson & Mapp, 2002; Patrikakou, Weissberg, & Rubenstein, 1999; Redding, 2000). Homework is a primary point of interface between the school and the home, and parents are best able to support the school's purposes for homework when they understand what is expected of students and their role in monitoring their children's homework. Consistency from teacher to teacher and across grade levels and subjects contributes to teachers', parents', and students' understanding of the school's purposes for homework and also reinforces students' formation of independent study habits.

Guidelines for Homework

Homework is most effective when it is used in ways proven to contribute most to student learning and student acquisition of independent study habits. Guidelines for effective homework are:

- Homework must be monitored and followed up.
- Teacher comments on homework are vital; graded homework that counts is most effective. Prompt return of homework by teacher is essential.
- Practice and preparation assignments are primarily the responsibility of the students to complete themselves.
- It is unrealistic to expect parents to play significant instructional roles with homework, especially at the upper grades (Grolnick et al., 1997).
- In the elementary grades, brief forms of parental involvement are desirable (especially those assignments that call for students to show or explain their work to parents and get their reactions).
- Assigning homework for punishment is inappropriate.

Computer-Based and Technology-Assisted Instruction

More and more, technology is used to individualize instruction, provide a well-organized presentation of material, offer feedback, and allow students to progress at their own rate. Computer-based instruction is successful when the program is carefully aligned with the same standards and objectives that the teacher is addressing within the designated unit of instruction. This requires the teacher to know the content of the computer program and to use it in concert with other modes of instruction. It also requires that the teacher check for mastery of objectives independent of the program's validation of mastery. When a computer program is successful, students are engaged, on task, and comfortable with the program and its navigation. The teacher travels about the room to assist students and monitor their work. When a student is in need of assistance from the teacher, the teacher provides curriculum-related activities to avoid "down time." In terms of classroom management, the students are taught to make orderly transitions to and from their computer stations.

Instruction: Teacher and Student

With technology-assisted instruction, the teacher uses computers and other technology tools as a seamless part of the learning activity. Students use word processing programs to write and edit their written work. They develop projects with presentation software. They use the internet as a source of information. All this requires clear direction to gather, organize, and present information. To make technology-assisted instruction fruitful, teachers must be trained in the use of the software and must be supported in integrating the technology into the routine of instruction. Technology can also be a great asset to teachers in their recordkeeping.

Teacher-Student Interaction

Teacher-student interactions include teacher praise for and reinforcement of positive student behavior and demonstration of learning as well as questioning techniques and discussion methods. Teacher-student interactions are social, instructional, and managerial. Social interaction has been found to be a particularly strong correlate of academic learning (Wang, Haertel, &Walberg, 1993), as it facilitates a bond of connection between the teacher and the students and increases each student's sense of belonging to the classroom group.

Grossier (1964) suggested six characteristics of good questions that teachers use in instructional interaction with students. The question should be: 1) clear, specific, to the point, delivered one at a time, with a cue to channel the student's response; 2) purposeful, aligned with the lesson's intent, often written in advance by the teacher; 3) brief; 4) natural, in simple language, conversational, appropriate to the level of the class, and with clarification of any new words; 5) sequenced, starting with questions of fact, integrated with previously-discussed material, then prompting students to refine or apply their understanding, using a variety of types from Bloom's taxonomy, moving toward connection of lesson elements; and 6) thought provoking, sufficiently strong to arouse interest, and designed to help students understand and analyze.

Rowe (1974; 1986) demonstrated the effectiveness of sufficient pausing by the teacher after asking a question before calling on a student. When the pause was extended from the typical one second or less to three to five seconds, the quality of responses improved dramatically. These effects were most dramatic with less-able students. Other studies have verified these conclusions (DeTure, 1979; Swift, Gooding, & Swift, 1988; Tobin, 1983).

Drill and recitation occur frequently in classrooms and are important instructional tools, but true group discussion is rare. Activities that teachers call "discussion" tend to be recitations in which teachers ask questions and students respond by reciting what they already know or are now learning. A true discussion involves teachers and students sharing ideas in order to clarify issues, relate new knowledge to their prior experience, or attempt to answer a question or solve a problem (Alvermann, O'Brien, & Dillon, 1990; Tharp & Gallimore, 1988).

The pace of a discussion is noticeably slower than a recitation; longer periods of silence are sustained between speakers. Sometimes questions can actually impede discussions. To avoid this, Dillon (1979) lists six alternatives to questioning that teachers can use to sustain discussions: 1) declarative statements; 2) declarative restatements that summarize a student's point; 3) indirect questions to avoid the sound of rejection and prompt more careful consideration; 4) imperatives, such as "tell us more about that" or "perhaps you could give us an example"; 5) student questions—asking for students to ask questions of other students; 6) deliberate silence to allow students to absorb content.

Classroom Culture

A meta-analysis of 28 factors that affect school learning (Wang, Haertel, & Walberg, 1993) found that the single most powerful factor is classroom management—the way the teacher organizes and manages the complex variables of curriculum, time, space, and interaction with students. Classroom management is evidenced in the teacher's "withitness," the learner's accountability for learning, the clear procedures in the classroom, and the way the teacher mixes whole-class instruction, small-group instruction, and individual instruction.

Consistent reinforcement of classroom rules and procedures is key to classroom management (Emmer et al., 1984; Evertson et al., 1984). Rules and procedures are posted in the classroom, and students are reminded of them and learn to operate according to them. The effective teacher "teaches" classroom procedures in a positive way rather than relying solely on correction of violations. Frequently resorting to correction and punishment is a sign of inadequate classroom management methods, but consistent enforcement of rules and procedures is a necessity (Stage & Quiroz, 1997).

Instruction: Teacher and Student

Teacher "withitness" is described by Brophy (1996) as the teacher being "aware of what is happening in all parts of the classroom at all times … by continuously scanning the classroom, even when working with small groups or individuals. Also [the teacher demonstrates] … this withitness by intervening promptly and accurately when inappropriate behavior threatens to become disruptive" (p. 11). The way a teacher plans, organizes, manages, and watches over the classroom determines the prevailing "culture." Students adopt the ethos of the classroom culture, responding to what the teacher has created and to the way the teacher behaves.

Whole-class instruction has been described in detail above, and the teacher exercises immediate control over the classroom culture during whole-class instruction, operating as the central character while interacting with the rest of the cast. The Whole-Class Instruction Plan guides the teacher in teaching in the whole-class mode. The Mega System distinguishes between two primary groupings within the classroom—Whole-Class Instruction and Work Time. Work Time is the classroom time when the teacher is not teaching the whole class, but students are learning in either an independent (individual) mode or in various small-group configurations. During Work Time, the teacher has an opportunity to individualize instruction by drawing from the learning plan grids for the unit to create Student Learning Plans to guide each student's activities. A Student Learning Plan is typically a one-week plan developed by the teacher for the class, with a variety of learning activities that enable the teacher to adapt the plan for individual students. One Student Learning Plan is developed for each subject area. The Student Learning Plan guides the student's activity during work time, is reviewed by parents when completed, and is then returned to the teacher to be maintained in the student's file. Learning activities are leveled (see objective levels in Learning Plan Grid) according to the student's evidence of prior learning, particularly on the unit pre-test and subsequent work within the unit of instruction.

The following pages show examples of Student Learning Plans for students who are able to read and follow directions. Simpler forms using symbols and colors work well with kindergarten and first-grade students. The Student Learning Plan is the teacher's vehicle for individualizing instruction and establishing a classroom culture that encourages student-directed work and accountability.

Student Learning Plan

Student's Name: _____ Teacher's Name: _____

Pre-Test Date: _____ Post-Test Date: _____ Subject: _____

Standards/Benchmarks Codes: _____ Objective Codes: _____ Week(s) of: _____

Sequence	Independent Activities (Check)	Centers	Homework (Circle)	Teacher Check
	Activity Number and Title	(Check) (Number AC)	Activity Number and Title	Initial/Date
1	___ 1) ___ 2) ___ 3) ___ 4)	AC ____ CC ____ EC ____	___ 1) ___ 2) ___ 3) ___ 4)	
2	___ 1) ___ 2) ___ 3) ___ 4)	AC ____ CC ____ EC ____	___ 1) ___ 2) ___ 3) ___ 4)	
3	___ 1) ___ 2) ___ 3) ___ 4)	AC ____ CC ____ EC ____	___ 1) ___ 2) ___ 3) ___ 4)	
4	___ 1) ___ 2) ___ 3) ___ 4)	AC ____ CC ____ EC ____	___ 1) ___ 2) ___ 3) ___ 4)	
5	___ 1) ___ 2) ___ 3) ___ 4)	AC ____ CC ____ EC ____	___ 1) ___ 2) ___ 3) ___ 4)	

Centers: AC = Activity Center and number of activity to complete; CC = Cooperative Center, EC = Exploratory Center
Activity Number and Title correspond with Activity Instructions.
Student: Draw line through completed activity. Teacher Check indicates that sequence was completed by student.

Teacher Comments: _____

Parent Comments: _____

Parent Signature: _____ Date: _____

Student Learning Plan (Class Example for Most Students)

Student's Name: _____ Teacher's Name: _____ Mrs. Hanger _____

Pre-Test Date: ___9-3-04___ Post-Test Date: ___10-2-04___ Subject: _____ Reading _____

Standards/Benchmarks Codes: __A3__ Objective Codes: __3R1-1 to 3R1-4__ Week(s) of: __Sept. 11, 2004__

Sequence	Independent Activities (Check)	Centers	Homework (Circle)	Teacher Check
	Activity Number and Title	(Check) (Number AC)	Activity Number and Title	Initial/Date
1	___ 1) What is a sentence p. 17 _X_ 2) Sentence structure p. 20, C&D ___ 3) Declarative and Inter. Sentences p. 24, A&B ___ 4)	AC _2_ CC ___ EC ___	___ 1) p. 3, 6-15 _X_ 2) p. 3, 16-20 ___ 3) p. 28, 19-25 Add Label words to make a sentence ___ 4)	
2	___ 1) Sentence punctuation p. 18, B _X_ 2) Imperative and Excl. p. 19, 2-10 ___ 3) Letter writing p. 25, C&D ___ 4) Booktime	AC _2_ CC _X_ EC ___	___ 1) p. 5, 13-20 Punctuation _X_ 2) p. 7, 8-15 Label sentences ___ 3) Finish letter ___ 4) Read for 20 minutes	
3	___ 1) Vocabulary building worksheet _X_ 2) Context clues worksheet ___ 3) Combining sentences worksheet ___ 4)	AC _2_ CC ___ EC ___	___ 1) p. 39, 1-6 Create sentences _X_ 2) p. 39, 7-11 ___ 3) p. 23, 6-12 Context clues/ combining ___ 4) Main Idea	
4	___ 1) Combining words p. 21 A _X_ 2) Vocabulary list of the week ___ 3) Parts of a story worksheet ___ 4)	AC _2_ CC ___ EC ___	___ 1) Where you would like to visit ___ 2) ___ 3) p. 55, 1-2 ___ 4)	
5	___ 1) Time-order words worksheet _X_ 2) Detail sentences p. 21 B ___ 3) Main idea worksheet ___ 4) Booktime	AC _2_ CC ___ EC _X_	___ 1) Paragraph using time-order words _X_ 2) p. 50, Write 4 detail ___ 3) p. 72, 1-6 Main Idea and details ___ 4) Read for 20 minutes	

Centers: AC = Activity Center and number of activity to complete; CC = Cooperative Center, EC = Exploratory Center
Activity Number and Title correspond with Activity Instructions.
Student: Draw line through completed activity. Teacher Check indicates that sequence was completed by student.

Teacher Comments: _____

Parent Comments: _____

Parent Signature: _____ Date: _____

Student Learning Plan (Example for a Student Not Initially Ready for Target Objectives)

Student's Name: _____ Teacher's Name: _____ Mrs. Hanger

Pre-Test Date: __9-3-04__ Post-Test Date: __10-2-04__ Subject: __Reading__

Standards/Benchmarks Codes: __A3__ Objective Codes: __3R1-1 to 3R1-4__ Week(s) of: __Sept. 11, 2004__

Sequence	Independent Activities (Check)	Centers	Homework (Circle)	Teacher Check
	Activity Number and Title	(Check) (Number AC)	Activity Number and Title	Initial/Date
1	X 1) What is a sentence p. 17 __ 2) Sentence structure p. 20, C&D C & D __ 3) Declarative and Inter. Sentences p. 24, A&B __ 4)	AC __1__ CC ____ EC ____	X 1) p. 3, 6-15 __ 2) p. 3, 16-20 __ 3) p. 28, 19-25 Add Label words to make a sentence __ 4)	
2	X 1) Sentence punctuation p. 18, B __ 2) Imperative and Excl. p. 19, 2-10 __ 3) Letter writing p. 25, C&D __ 4) Booktime	AC __1__ CC __X__ EC ____	__ 1) p. 5, 13-20 Punctuation X 2) p. 7, 8-15 Label sentences __ 3) Finish letter __ 4) Read for 20 minutes	
3	X 1) Vocabulary building worksheet X 2) Context clues worksheet __ 3) Combining sentences worksheet __ 4)	AC __1__ CC ____ EC ____	__ 1) p. 39, 1-6 Create sentences X 2) p. 39, 7-11 __ 3) p. 23, 6-12 Context clues/ combining __ 4) Main Idea	
4	__ 1) Combining words p. 21 A X 2) Vocabulary list of the week __ 3) Parts of a story worksheet __ 4)	AC __2__ CC ____ EC ____	X 1) Where you would like to visit __ 2) __ 3) p. 55, 1-2 __ 4)	
5	__ 1) Time-order words worksheet X 2) Detail sentences p. 21 B __ 3) Main idea worksheet __ 4) Booktime	AC __2__ CC ____ EC ____	__ 1) Paragraph using time-order words X 2) p. 50, Write 4 detail __ 3) p. 72, 1-6 Main Idea and details __ 4) Read for 20 minutes	

Centers: AC = Activity Center and number of activity to complete; CC = Cooperative Center, EC = Exploratory Center Activity Number and Title correspond with Activity Instructions.
Student: Draw line through completed activity. Teacher Check indicates that sequence was completed by student.

Teacher Comments: _____

Parent Comments: _____

Parent Signature: _____ Date: _____

Student Learning Plan (Example for a Student Demonstrating Early Mastery)

Student's Name: _____ Teacher's Name: _____ Mrs. Hanger _____

Pre-Test Date: __9-3-04__ Post-Test Date: ___10-2-04___ Subject: _____Reading_____

Standards/Benchmarks Codes: __A3__ Objective Codes: __3R1-1 to 3R1-4__ Week(s) of: __Sept. 11, 2004__

Sequence	Independent Activities (Check)	Centers	Homework (Circle)	Teacher Check
	Activity Number and Title	(Check) (Number AC)	Activity Number and Title	Initial/Date
1	__ 1) *What is a sentence p. 17* X 2) *Sentence structure p. 20, C&D* X 3) *Declarative and Inter. Sentences p. 24, A&B* __ 4)	AC _2_ CC ___ EC ___	__ 1) *p. 3, 6-15* X 2) *p. 3, 16-20* __ 3) *p. 28, 19-25 Add Label words to make a sentence* __ 4)	
2	__ 1) *Sentence punctuation p. 18, B* __ 2) *Imperative and Excl. p. 19, 2-10* X 3) *Letter writing p. 25, C&D* __ 4) *Booktime*	AC _3_ CC _X_ EC ___	__ 1) *p. 5, 13-20 Punctuation* __ 2) *p. 7, 8-15 Label sentences* X 3) *Finish letter* __ 4) *Read for 20 minutes*	
3	__ 1) *Vocabulary building worksheet* X 2) *Context clues worksheet* __ 3) *Combining sentences worksheet* __ 4)	AC _3_ CC ___ EC ___	__ 1) *p. 39, 1-6 Create sentences* X 2) *p. 39, 7-11* __ 3) *p. 23, 6-12 Context clues/combining* __ 4) *Main Idea*	
4	__ 1) *Combining words p. 21 A* __ 2) *Vocabulary list of the week* X 3) *Parts of a story worksheet* __ 4)	AC _3_ CC ___ EC ___	__ 1) *Where you would like to visit* __ 2) X 3) *p. 55, 1-2* __ 4)	
5	__ 1) *Time-order words worksheet* __ 2) *Detail sentences p. 21 B* X 3) *Main idea worksheet* X 4) *Booktime*	AC _3_ CC ___ EC ___	__ 1) *Paragraph using time-order words* __ 2) *p. 50, Write 4 detail* X 3) *p. 72, 1-6 Main Idea and details* __ 4) *Read for 20 minutes*	

Centers: AC = Activity Center and number of activity to complete; CC = Cooperative Center, EC = Exploratory Center
Activity Number and Title correspond with Activity Instructions.
Student: Draw line through completed activity. Teacher Check indicates that sequence was completed by student.

Teacher Comments: _____

Parent Comments: _____

Parent Signature: _____ Date: _____

Targeted Learning

"Targeted learning" is a term applied to instruction that is ideal for the individual student, taking into account that student's prior mastery. Targeted learning contributes to the student's motivation to learn because the student perceives learning tasks as challenging but not forbidding. Targeted learning models and encourages personal responsibility for learning and the application of a variety of strategies to reach successful ends. As previously described, the teacher assesses students routinely and periodically to make the most appropriate assignment of new learning tasks. The teacher selects from a variety of instructional modes to build the student's ability to apply various learning strategies, thus enhancing metacognitive skills, and to maintain a high level of interest. From a strong presentational base in well-executed, whole-class instruction, targeted learning proceeds to reach each student individually, bringing that student to mastery of standards-based objectives. While targeted learning provides prerequisite steps to mastery for some students, it also enhances learning beyond the level of the standard for other students, thus making the standards-based objective a floor and not a ceiling. Because each student is assessed for each objective, no student is consigned to a "group" or "track," but is able to reach and exceed each objective based on the student's demonstrated readiness for and mastery of that particular objective.

Student Motivation to Learn

Student motivation to learn depends upon the student's perceived self-efficacy in the face of a learning challenge, and the teacher's interaction with students affects perceived self-efficacy over time. Albert Bandura (1997, p. 3) defines self-efficacy perception as "beliefs in one's capabilities to organize and execute the courses of action required to produce given attainments." When a student approaches a new learning task, the student's perception of his or her ability to successfully complete the task bears on the motivation to persist with the task. Self-efficacy influences academic motivation, learning, and achievement (Pajares, 1996; Schunk, 1995; Schunk & Pajares, 2002). A student's self-efficacy perception, the anticipation of success, is derived from the student's assessment of his or her own level of skill and the relative challenge of the task at hand (Csikszentmihalyi, 1990; 1993). When perceived skill is high and the challenge low, the student is bored. When perceived skill is low and the challenge high, the student becomes anxious and prone to avoid the task. The job of the teacher is to set learning tasks that are suf-

Instruction: Teacher and Student

ficiently challenging for the student while within the proximate reach of the student's abilities. The skillful teacher heightens the student's interest and perception of likely success. This is the essence of targeted learning—planning learning tasks for each student that are appropriate to that student's demonstrated prior knowledge and provided in an instructional mode that heightens the student's interest, value for the result, and perception of likely success.

A teacher can increase a student's perception of self-efficacy, thus elevating the student's effort, persistence, and ultimate level of performance by: 1) encouraging students to set goals that are specific, challenging, but attainable, 2) modeling effective responses to tasks, 3) providing feedback that encourages students to stay on course until achieving mastery, and 4) making attributional statements that help students understand and appreciate that they are improving their own abilities by accepting challenges and maintaining effort (Bandura, 1997; Schunk & Ertmer, 2000).

Motivation is something we can only detect indirectly; we assume from a student's willingness to tackle a new task and persist with it that the student is "motivated" toward it. Motivation is a theoretical construct that we employ in order to explain goal-directed behavior (Maehr & Meyer, 1997). In fact, all behavior is motivated to some extent. Teachers want students to be motivated to learn. In the classroom context, the concept of student motivation is used to explain the degree to which students invest attention and effort in various pursuits, which may or may not be the ones desired by teachers. Thus, it is not fair to say that a student lacks motivation when, in fact, the student is motivated by something other than what the teacher desires. The trick is to encourage student motivation toward learning objectives.

It is unrealistic to expect teachers to teach and students to learn motivated purely by intrinsic factors. Interest leading to play or casual exploration is not the same as motivated and focused learning. If students think of an activity as play rather than as learning, they will not use the processes needed to get the most out of the experience and file it away for future application. Students may be motivated to learn from an activity whether or not they find its content interesting or its process enjoyable. They may not get to choose the activity, but they can choose to get the most out of it (Brophy, 2004, p. 250).

Even if the student does not find the topic of high interest, the student will persist with the learning task if the topic (or the acquisition of the skill or knowledge) is perceived as valuable.

Kieran Egan (2002) makes a similar point when he distinguishes between learning "in nature," the incidental learning that occurs naturally as part of a child's playing and interacting with the world around him, and the formal learning in school which requires focus, discipline, and concerted effort. Even the acquisition of language, which Egan explains occurs with miraculous ease because of the brain's innate cognitive structures for it, is something apart from school learning.

When the topic is of high interest to a student, that level of interest may provide intrinsic motivation for the student to pursue the subject. But some topics are not of high interest to every student, and yet it is essential that the student learn about them. The process of learning—careful listening and reading, studying to master and memorize, practicing—can, in fact, be quite tedious. Depending upon the teacher's enthusiasm and the topic's interest, it is not always enough to "motivate" students to learn. Students must be encouraged to be motivated by learning itself (Brophy, 2004). In other words, the student finds reward in the acquisition of new skills and knowledge. Anticipating the satisfaction of accomplishment, the student is motivated to persist, even if the topic is not of great initial interest and the task of mastery is arduous.

The value a student places on learning contributes to the student's mental calculus in approaching a new task. Even if the student does not find the topic of high interest, the student will persist with the learning task if the topic (or the acquisition of the skill or knowledge) is perceived as valuable. The classic example of perceived value is found in the attention high school sophomores give to mastering the material necessary to acquire a driver's license. Learning the rules of the road may not be a topic of high interest, but success in learning them is of great value to the student who wants to drive.

The teacher contributes to a student's desire to learn by modeling an enthusiasm for learning and for the specific topic; presenting material clearly, interactively, and directly; interacting socially and academically with students; and allowing students a degree of self-direction or self-management of their learning toward clear objectives. Students respond to the right blend of caring and expectation, the knowledge that the teacher "knows me and thinks there is something special about me," recognition for accomplishment derived from evidence of effort and mastery, the opportunity to manage work tasks and to be responsible for them, and content that is challenging and interestingly presented.

Instruction: Teacher and Student

The effective teacher scaffolds each students' learning with clear goals, advance organizers, skillful questioning, and targeted learning activities. Reluctant and apathetic students must be resocialized to alter their attitudes and behaviors by developing a close working relationship with them, building upon their existing knowledge and interests, and intentionally expecting their positive attitude toward schoolwork.

While the teacher models enthusiasm for learning and the topic at hand, enthusiasm does not mean pep talks and phony theatrics. It means genuine personal delight in learning, identifying good reasons to view a topic as interesting, meaningful, and important. The purpose is not to amuse or entertain, but to induce students to value the topic or activity. All students, but especially at-risk students, do best with teachers who:

> share warm, personal interactions with them but also hold high expectations for their academic progress, require them to perform up to their capabilities, and see that they progress as far and as fast as they are able. These teachers break through social-class differences, cultural differences, language differences, and other potential barriers to communication in order to form close relationships with at-risk students, but they use these relationships to maximize the students' academic progress, not merely to provide friendship or sympathy to them (Brophy, 2004, p. 360).

At-risk students are especially successful when they feel a bond with their teacher and classmates, and such bonding is achieved by establishing a warm and inviting social climate. Respect for each student's background of language and tradition is essential in creating a trusting classroom environment. The teacher who visits homes, knows students' familial milieu, and shows respect for what the student brings to the classroom will contribute greatly to each student's desire to learn.

Helping students articulate their own aspirations also reinforces the attitudes conducive to learning, placing a healthy emphasis on what the student wants to become. Knowledge itself equips the mind to learn in new and different ways. Categorizing students by suspected learning styles is a form of pigeonholing. It limits what a child learns, which in turn limits what a child is capable of learning. A child is best served by encouraging the exercise of a variety of learning strategies.

THE LANGUAGE OF METACOGNITION

Teachers talk the language of metacognition by thinking out loud, helping students see the possible routes to mastery of new concepts and skills, and encouraging self-direction and responsibility for mastery.

Metacognition

Metacognition is thinking about thinking, the learner's ability to know what he or she knows and to adapt learning strategies in order to reach desired ends. Teachers help students build their metacognitive awareness and skills by showing the roadmap of learning, enabling them to see learning objectives as their personal goals. Teachers talk the language of metacognition by thinking out loud, helping students see the possible routes to mastery of new concepts and skills, and encouraging self-direction and responsibility for mastery. The mix of instructional modes and variety of learning activities acquaints students with the repertoire of strategies that might be applied to any learning situation. In addition, the teacher directly teaches students efficient methods for approaching, comprehending, mastering, and sometimes memorizing material within the context of the objectives at hand. Teaching metacognitive and critical thinking skills apart from subject matter is ineffective, and teachers are most successful when they embed this important component of learning within the curriculum.

It is important to reiterate that learning strategies should not be confused with learning styles. Most learning style research has been done in limited areas of the curriculum and with very mixed, negative, and unconvincing results. Advocates of learning styles tend also to overlook the advice of creditable researchers for teachers to "help students to 'stretch' to function in the learning modes they use infrequently" (Brophy, 2004, p. 342).

Learning style schemes and over-differentiation of instruction according to "cognitive styles" lack research validation. While it is wise to offer more than one route to mastery and to teach different subjects in different ways, teachers should avoid round-about means to achieve learning ends, labeling and stereotyping students, and overemphasis of perceived student strengths without sufficient attention to weaknesses (Krechevsky & Seidel, 2001). The central purpose of schooling is for children to learn what they don't already know, grow in areas where they lack development, and expand their areas of interest and knowledge.

Instruction: Teacher and Student

Brophy (2004) cautions against capitulation to perceived student preferences as opposed to balanced development of a menu of learning strategies and modes:

> In order to attain certain learning goals students must engage in processes that they might prefer to avoid (presentations to the class, debates, cooperative work on a group project). Or you might have to limit certain students' opportunities to pursue favorite topics or learn in their preferred mode, because if the students spent too much time indulging these preferences they would fail to develop knowledge or skills needed in school or in life generally. (p. 345)

Teaching and modeling a metacognitive approach to learning benefits students. The teacher shows students how to address a learning task by:

- Defining the task: What am I expected to learn and what do I already know?
- Goal-setting: How will I know when I have completed the task? What strategies will I apply?
- Applying learning strategies: Research, practice, ask questions, memorize, outline, other strategies.
- Monitoring: What new information do I need? Is this a simple or difficult task? How do I approach it? How am I doing? Should I try a different strategy?

Learning strategies are applied at each point within a *learning cycle*, as diagramed below:

Learning Cycle

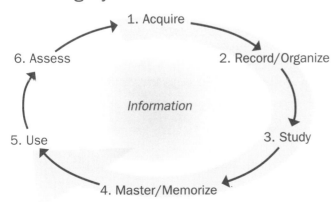

1. Acquire
2. Record/Organize
3. Study
4. Master/Memorize
5. Use
6. Assess

Information

Instruction: Teacher and Student

Teachers help students build metacognitive skills by:

- Connecting new learning to prior learning.
- Helping students focus on what is expected and HOW to meet those expectations.
- Articulating expectations clearly.
- Modeling and demonstrating strategies for mastery.
- Showing students how to "check" their own mastery.
- Breaking complicated processes into simpler steps.
- Helping students focus on mastery rather than fear of failing.
- Helping students find their own errors and self-correct.
- Emphasizing learning, task mastery, and effort rather than ability, performance, and competition.

Attribution

To what does a student attribute his/her learning success or difficulty? The answer affects both motivation and metacognition. Constructive attributions include effort, strategies applied, and available information: "I need to try harder, try a different approach, ask questions." Lack of ability is a destructive attribution: "I'm just not smart enough." Equally non-productive are deflective attributions which externalize the source of difficulty: "It's not about me. The teacher doesn't like me. The test isn't fair." Even when students are successful, they may express counterproductive attributions: "The test was easy." "The teacher likes me." "I was just lucky." Through their interactions with students, teachers give signals that reinforce attributions. Asking key questions and shaping the acceptable responses helps students view learning as a process over which they exercise considerable control: "What do you think you need to do to reach this objective?" "Why do you think you did so well?" By targeting instruction for each student, the teacher paves a path of possibility that encourages constructive attribution. By modeling metacognitive skills, the teacher emphasizes the learner's active role in learning, discouraging external attribution for success and failure.

Professional Development

Professional development in the Mega System parallels the school improvement plan and evidence of research-based practices in the classroom. When the school improvement plan calls for new expertise to enable the school to move in a new direction or to address a particular problem, professional development is a means for elevating the skill and knowledge of administrators, teachers, and staff. When classroom observations by the principal or other teachers (as in peer observation and collegial learning) indicate a general need for improvement across the faculty, well-planned professional development is a way to improve. When classroom observations by the principal or another teacher show an individual teacher's areas that need improvement, that teacher's personal development plan can include training or coaching to assist the teacher in the area of need.

The list of indicators of research-based instructional practices at the end of this chapter provides the basis for a rubric for classroom observations. The principal or another teacher would meet with the observed teacher before the observation to review the indicators and again after the observation to discuss the observer's impressions. The teacher and the observer then create or update a professional development plan for the teacher, listing: a) observed strengths and ways the teacher might share his/her expertise with other teachers, and b) areas that need improvement and steps toward improvement. The observer assists the teacher in carrying out these next steps.

Continuous improvement of each teacher's skills is achieved through a variety of means including whole-faculty workshops, consultations with Instructional Teams, the principal's work with individual teachers and with teams, and through collegial learning— teacher to teacher (including peer observations, study groups, coaching, and mentoring). While teacher evaluation is something apart from professional development, evaluation should include examination of the teacher's proficiency with the same indicators used to plan professional development for each individual teacher and for the faculty as whole.

Professional Development

The Professional Development Plan for Teachers on the next page provides a post-observation agenda for a meeting between the observer and the teacher as well as an action plan and record of the meeting's conclusions. This plan is premised upon one or more observations of the teacher using a checklist of research-based indicators such as those provided later in this chapter. Analysis of the plans for all teachers provides guidance in providing professional development targeted to areas in need of improvement across the faculty. The areas of strength outlined in the plan create an inventory of expertise within the faculty, useful in pairing teachers for coaching and in selecting teachers to lead workshop sessions and study groups.

Professional Development Plan for Teachers

Teacher's Name: _____

You will need a copy of the completed Classroom Observation Instrument.

Identified below are the three top areas of strengths and three areas that most indicate a need for improvement based on the Classroom Observation Instrument.

Indicators	Strengths Ways to Share Expertise	Timeline to Completion
1.		
2.		
3.		

Indicators	Areas to be Improved Strategies To Be Used	Timeline to Completion
1.		
2.		
3.		

Teacher's Signature: _____ **Date:** _____

Observer's Signature: _____ **Date:** _____

Chapter Summary

Chapter 2 outlined decision-making structures through which learning data are analyzed. Chapter 3 has covered the bases of learning—curriculum, assessment, instruction, and professional development—providing a review of evidence on effective approaches to each. We have established a framework within which a school can guide and monitor its progress and the progress of each of its students. We have offered a distillation of research on curriculum, assessment, and instruction, generalized to apply across grade levels and subject areas. Within each subject area, and for each grade or age level, more specific research will guide the teacher. A framework for school improvement, however, seeks general application of sound practices and monitors both these practices and their outcomes, adjusting course in response to the data. The Mega System includes both decision-making structures to guide and monitor progress and sound instructional practices most likely to achieve the desired results. While a model would measure progress against implementation standards, a system measures progress by accomplishment of results in student learning.

Putting Learning Components in Place

The forms on the following pages may be used to assess the current status of key elements of a learning system and to plan for the development of the missing pieces. A Leadership Team can work through these forms, develop a plan of action, and monitor the progress. For items checked "No" on the assessment of the current situation, primary responsibility is assigned to a person or team, with an expected date for completion of the task. Many of the items are worded to apply to "the teacher." This makes these items useful for classroom observations by the principal, peer observations between teachers, and self-assessment by individual teachers. For the purpose of determining the current status of these indicators within the school, the Leadership Team should consider the extent to which each indicator could be awarded a "yes" for *all* teachers. Periodically, a compilation of observations of or self-assessments by all teachers can be produced, without reference to individual teachers' names, to show the strength of the indicator in the school. This information is especially useful in planning professional development.

Learning Indicators

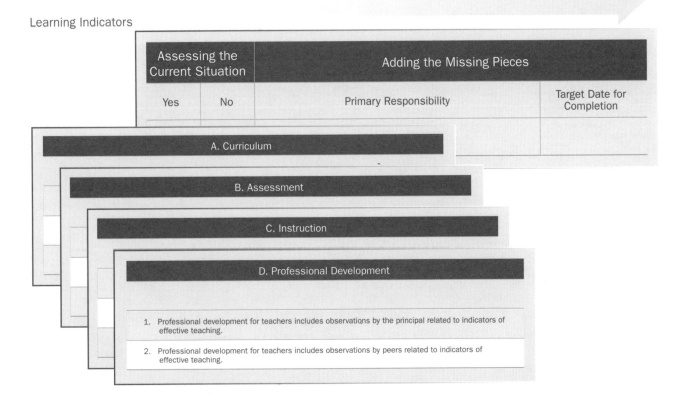

Assessing the Current Situation		Adding the Missing Pieces	
Yes	No	Primary Responsibility	Target Date for Completion

A. Curriculum

B. Assessment

C. Instruction

D. Professional Development

1. Professional development for teachers includes observations by the principal related to indicators of effective teaching.

2. Professional development for teachers includes observations by peers related to indicators of effective teaching.

Learning Indicators

A. Curriculum

1. Instructional Teams develop standards-aligned units of instruction for each subject and grade level.

2. Teachers are guided by a document that aligns standards, curriculum, instruction, and assessment.

3. Teachers submit weekly lesson plans based on aligned units of instruction.

4. Units of instruction include standards-based objectives and criteria for mastery.

5. Units of instruction include pre/post tests to assess student mastery.

6. Units of instruction include specific learning activities aligned to objectives.

7. Instructional Teams develop materials for their standards-aligned learning activities and share the materials among themselves.

8. Materials for standards-aligned learning activities are well-organized, labeled, and stored for convenient use by teachers.

B. Assessment

The teacher:

1. Uses objectives-based pre-tests.

2. Uses objectives-based post-tests.

3. Maintains a record of each student's mastery of specific learning objectives.

4. Tests frequently using a variety of evaluation methods and maintains a record of the results.

5. Differentiates assignments in response to individual student performance on pre-tests and other methods of assessment.

Assessing the Current Situation		Adding the Missing Pieces		
Yes	No		Primary Responsibility	Target Date for Completion

Assessing the Current Situation		Adding the Missing Pieces		
Yes	No		Primary Responsibility	Target Date for Completion

Learning Indicators

C. Instruction	
Classroom Culture	
1. When waiting for assistance from the teacher, students are occupied with curriculum-related activities provided by the teacher.	
2. Transitions between instructional modes are brief and orderly.	
3. Students maintain eye contact and are attentive.	
4. Students raise hands or otherwise signal before speaking.	
The teacher:	
5. Uses a variety of instructional modes—whole-class, small-group, independent, computer-assisted, computer-based.	
6. Maintains well-organized student learning materials in the classroom.	
7. Displays completed student work in the classroom.	
8. Posts classroom rules and procedures in the classroom.	
9. Corrects students who do not follow classroom rules and procedures.	
10. Reinforces classroom rules and procedures by positively teaching them.	
11. Conducts an occasional "behavior check."	
12. Engages all students, e.g., encourages silent students to participate.	
13. Is active in the classroom regardless of the instructional mode.	
14. Interacts with students socially, instructionally, and managerial as appropriate.	

Assessing the Current Situation		Adding the Missing Pieces	
Yes	No	Primary Responsibility	Target Date for Completion

Learning Indicators

C. Instruction *(continued)*	
Teacher-Directed Whole-Class or Small Group: Introduction	
The teacher:	
1. Reviews the previous lesson.	
2. Clearly states the lesson's topic, theme, objectives.	
3. Stimulates interest in the topics.	
4. Uses modeling, demonstration, graphics.	
Teacher-Directed Whole-Class or Small Group: Presentation	
The teacher:	
1. Proceeds in small steps at rapid pace.	
2. Explains directly and thoroughly.	
3. Maintains eye contact.	
4. Speaks with expression and uses a variety of vocal tones.	
5. Uses prompting/cueing.	
Teacher-Directed Whole-Class or Small-Group: Summarize/Confirm Mastery	
The teacher:	
1. Re-teaches when necessary.	
2. Reviews with drilling/class recitation.	
3. Reviews with questioning.	
4. Summarizes key concepts.	

Assessing the Current Situation			Adding the Missing Pieces	
	Yes	No	Primary Responsibility	Target Date for Completion

Learning Indicators

C. Instruction *(continued)*	
Teacher-Directed Whole-Class or Small Group: Teacher-Student Interaction	
The teacher:	
1. Re-teaches following questioning.	
2. Uses open-ended questioning and encourages elaboration.	
3. Re-directs student questions.	
4. Encourages peer interaction.	
5. Encourages students to paraphrase, summarize, relate.	
6. Encourages students to check their own comprehension.	
7. Verbally praises students.	
Student-Directed Small-Group or Independent	
The teacher:	
1. Travels to all areas in which students are working.	
2. Meets with students to facilitate mastery of objectives.	
3. Encourages students to help each other with their work.	
4. Interacts instructionally with students (explaining, checking, giving feedback).	
5. Interacts managerially with students (reinforcing rules, procedures).	
6. Interacts socially with students (noticing and attending to an ill student, asking about the weekend, inquiring about the family).	
7. Verbally praises students.	

	Assessing the Current Situation		Adding the Missing Pieces	
	Yes	No	Primary Responsibility	Target Date for Completion

Learning Indicators

C. Instruction *(continued)*	
Computer-Based Instruction	
1. Students are engaged and on task.	
2. Students are comfortable with the program and its navigation.	
The teacher:	
3. Travels about the room to assist students.	
4. Has documentation of the computer program's alignment with standards-based objectives.	
5. Maintains a record of student mastery of standards-based objectives.	
6. Assesses student mastery in ways other than those provided by the computer program.	
Homework, Communication with Parents	
The teacher:	
1. Maintains a file of communication with parents.	
2. Regularly assigns homework (4 or more days a week).	
3. Checks, marks, and returns homework.	
4. Includes comments on checked homework.	
5. Counts homework toward the student's report card grade.	
6. Systematically reports to parents the student's mastery of specific objectives.	

Assessing the Current Situation		Adding the Missing Pieces	
Yes	No	Primary Responsibility	Target Date for Completion

Learning Indicators

D. Professional Development	
1. Professional development for teachers includes observations by the principal related to indicators of effective teaching.	
2. Professional development for teachers includes observations by peers related to indicators of effective teaching.	
3. Professional development for teachers includes self-assessment related to indicators of effective teaching.	
4. Teachers are required to make individual professional development plans based, in part, on classroom observations.	
5. Professional development of individual teachers includes an emphasis on indicators of effective teaching.	
6. Professional development for the whole faculty includes assessment of strengths and areas in need of improvement from classroom observations of indicators of effective teaching.	
7. Teacher evaluation examines the same indicators used in professional development.	
8. The principal plans opportunities for teachers to share their strengths with other teachers.	

Assessing the Current Situation		Adding the Missing Pieces	
Yes	No	Primary Responsibility	Target Date for Completion

Chapter 3 References

Alexander, P. A., Kulikowich, J. M., & Schulze, S. K. (1994). How subject matter knowledge affects recall and interest. *American Educational Research Journal, 31*(2), 313-337.

Alvermann, D. E., O'Brien, D. G., & Dillon, D. R. (1990). What teachers do when they say they're having discussions of content area reading assignments: A qualitative analysis. *Reading Research Quarterly, 25*(4), 296-322.

Anderson, L., & Pigford, A. (1988). Teaching within-classroom groups: Examining the role of the teacher. *Journal of Classroom Interaction, 23*(2), 8-13.

Ausubel, D. (1968). *Educational psychology: A cognitive view.* New York: Holt, Rinehart & Winston.

Bandura, A. (1997). *Self-efficacy: The exercise of control.* New York: Freeman.

Brophy, J. E. (1996). *Teaching problem students.* New York: Guilford.

Brophy, J. E. (2004). *Motivating students to learn.* Mahwah, NJ: Lawrence Erlbaum.

Brophy, J. E., & Good, T. G. (1986). Teacher behavior and student achievement. In M. Wittrock (Ed.), *Handbook of research in teaching* (3rd ed., pp. 328–375). New York: Macmillan.

Csikszentmihalyi, M. (1990). *Flow: The psychology of optimal experience.* New York: Harper & Row.

Csikszentmihalyi, M. (1993). *The evolving self: A psychology for the third millennium.* New York: Harper Collins.

DeTure, L. (1979). Relative effects of modeling on the acquisition of wait-time by preservice elementary teachers and concomitant changes in dialogue patterns. *Journal of Research in Science Teaching, 16,* 553-562.

Dillon, J. (1979). Alternatives to questioning. *High School Journal, 62,* 217-222.

Eder, D., & Felmlee, D. (1984). Development of attention norms in ability groups. In P. Peterson, L. Wilkinson, & M. Hallinan (Eds.), *The social context of instruction: Group organization and group processes.* Orlando, FL: Academic Press.

Egan, K. (2002). *Getting it wrong from the beginning.* New Haven, CT: Yale University Press.

Emmer, E. T., Evertson, C. M., Sanford, J. P., Clements, B. S., & Worsham, M. E. (1984). *Classroom management for secondary teachers.* Englewood Cliffs, NJ: Prentice-Hall.

Epstein, J. L. (1995). School/family/community partnerships: Caring for the children we share. *Phi Delta Kappan, 76*(9), 701-712.

Evertson, C. M., Emmer, E. T., Clements, B. S., Sanford, J. P., & Worsham, M. E. (1984). *Classroom management for elementary teachers*. Englewood Cliffs, NJ: Prentice-Hall.

Good, T. (1996). Teacher effectiveness and teacher evaluation. In J. Sikula, T. Buttery, & E. Guyton (Eds.), *Handbook of research on teacher education* (2nd ed., pp. 617-665). New York: MacMillan.

Good, T. L., & Brophy, J. E. (2000). *Looking in classrooms* (8th ed.). New York: Addison Wesley Longman, Inc.

Glatthorn, A. (1995). *Developing a quality curriculum*. Alexandria, VA: Association for Supervision and Curriculum Development.

Grolnick, W. S., Kurowski, C. O., & Apostoleris, N. H. (1997). Predictors of parent involvement in children's schooling. *Journal of Educational Psychology, 89*(3), 538-548.

Grossier, P. (1964). *How to use the fine art of questioning*. New York: Teachers' Practical Press.

Haller, E. J. (1985). Pupil race and elementary school ability grouping: Are teachers biased against black children? *American Educational Research Journal, 22,* 465-483.

Hallinan, M. T., & Sorensen, A. B. (1985). Ability grouping and student friendships. *American Educational Research Journal, 22,* 485-499.

Henderson, A., & Mapp. K. (2002). *A new wave of evidence: The impact of school, family, and community connections on student achievement*. Austin, TX: Southwest Educational Development Laboratory.

Krechevsky, M., & Seidel, S. (2001). Minds at work: Applying multiple intelligences. In J. Collins & D. Cook (Eds.), *Understanding learning influences and outcomes*. London: The Open University.

Marzano, R. J. (2003). *What works in schools: Translating research into action*. Alexandria, VA: Association for Supervision & Curriculum Development.

Mason, D., & Good, T. (1993). Effects of two-group and whole-class teaching on regrouped elementary students' mathematics achievement. *American Educational Research Journal, 30,* 328-360.

Maehr, M. I., & Meyer, H. A. (1997). Understanding motivation and schooling: Where we've been, where we are, and where we need to go. *Educational Psychology Review, 9,* 371-409.

National Academy of Science. (1996). *National science education standards*. Washington, DC: National Academy Press.

Pajares, F. (1996). Self-efficacy beliefs in academic settings. *Review of Educational Research, 66,* 543-578.

Chapter 3 References (continued)

Patrikakou, E. N., Weissberg, R. P., & Rubenstein, M. (1999). School–family partnerships. In A. J. Reynolds, H. J. Walberg, & R. P. Weissberg (Eds.), *Promoting positive outcomes* (pp. 95-127). Washington, DC: Child Welfare League of America.

Redding, S. (2000). *Parents and learning*. Geneva: UNESCO Publications.

Reynolds, A. (1992). What is competent beginning teaching? A review of the literature. *Review of Educational Research, 62*, 1-35.

Rosenholtz, S. J. (1991). *Teacher's workplace: The social organization of schools.* New York: Teachers College Press.

Rosenshine, B. (1968). To explain: A review of research. *Educational Leadership, 26*, 275-280.

Rowan, S., & Miracle, A. (1983). Systems of ability grouping and the stratification of achievement in elementary schools. *Sociology of Education, 56*, 133-144.

Rowe, M. (1986). Wait time: Slowing down may be a way of speeding up! *Journal of Teacher Education, 37*, 43-50.

Rowe, M. (1974). Wait time and rewards as instructional variables, their influence on language, logic, and fate control: Part I–Wait time. *Journal of Research in Science Teaching, 11*, 81-94.

Schunk, D. H. (1995). Self-efficacy and education and instruction. In J. E. Maddux (Ed.), *Self-efficacy, adaptation, and adjustment: Theory, research, and application* (pp. 281-303). New York: Plenum Press.

Schunk, D. H., & Ertmer, P. A. (2000). Self-efficacy and academic learning: Self-efficacy enhancing interventions. In M. Boekaerts, P. R. Pintrich, & M. Zeidner (Eds.), *Handbook of self-regulation* (pp. 631-650). San Diego: Academic Press.

Schunk, D. H., & Pajares, F. (2002). The development of academic self-efficacy. In A. Wigfield & J. Eccles (Eds.), *Development of achievement motivation* (pp. 16-31). San Diego: Academic Press.

Stage, S. A., & Quiroz, D. R. (1997). A meta-analysis of interventions to decrease disruptive classroom behavior in public education settings. *School Psychology Review, 26*(3), 333-368.

Stone, C. L. (1983). A meta-analysis of advanced organizer studies. *Journal of Experimental Education, 51*(7), 194-199.

Swift, J., Gooding, C., & Swift, P. (1988). Questions and wait time. In J. Dillon (Ed.), *Questioning and discussion: A multidisciplinary study* (pp. 192-212). Norwood, NJ: Ablex.

Tobin, K. (1983). The influence of wait-time on classroom learning. *European Journal of Science Education, 5*(1), 35-48.

Tharp, R., & Gallimore, R. (1988). *Rousing minds to life: Teaching, learning, and schooling in social context.* Cambridge, MA: Cambridge University Press.

Walberg, H. J. (1984). Improving the productivity of America's schools. *Educational Leadership, 41*(8), 19-27.

Walberg, H. J. (1999). Productive teaching. In H. C. Waxman & H. J. Walberg (Eds.), *New directions for teaching practice and research* (pp. 75-104). Berkeley, CA: McCutchen Publishing Corporation.

Walberg, H. J., & Jin-Shei Lai. (1999). Meta-analytic effects for policy. In G. J. Cizek (Ed.), *Handbook of educational policy* (pp. 419-453). San Diego, CA: Academic Press.

Wang, M. C., Haertel, G. D., & Walberg, H. J. (1993). Toward a knowledge base for school learning. *Review of Educational Research, 63,* 249-294.

Waxman, H. C., & Walberg, H. J. (Eds.). (1991). *Effective teaching: Current research.* Berkeley, CA: McCutchan.

Weinstein, R. (1976). Reading group membership in first grade: Teacher behaviors and pupil experience over time. *Journal of Educational Psychology, 68*, 103-116.

Connecting–The School as Community

Isn't it interesting that schooling, where children come to know the world, is described with the terminology of big business, government bureaucracy, and the military? Models, systems, processes, structures, and outcomes are concepts applied to schooling but borrowed from the lexicon of large, formal organizations, which are typically devoted to products less tender than the hearts and minds of children. This is not a new phenomenon, but one whose beginning coincides with the emergence of the public school system in America in the nineteenth century. From the pluralistic irregularities of single schools operated by headmasters grew multi-school districts, state credentialing, and standardization of curriculum within each state. With complexity came the requirement for management, and management depends upon quantification, the measurement of processes and outcomes, and hierarchical chains of decision-making. The modern school district and state systems of education came of age along with the blooming of industrialism in America, and in time education adopted industry's methods of management, placing them within the regulatory protocols of government bureaucracy.

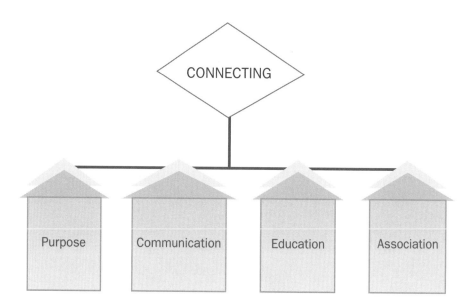

In the long march toward managed systems of schooling, there have been voices lamenting the loss of *Gemeinschaft*, the face-to-face bonds of community that might be found in less formal organizations. In fact, some observers attribute the inadequacies of public schooling to the invasion of scientific management and the abandonment of the gentler virtues of caring and personal commitment to shared values in children's acculturation (Sergiovanni, 1999). Likewise, American education never fully shed vestiges of its roots, maintaining stubborn adherence to local control of schools and democratic participation in limited aspects of school governance.

Making the case that parochial schools produce greater outcomes for less cost than public schools, even controlling for the socio-economic status of students, James Coleman (1987; 1990; Coleman & Hoffer, 1987) attributed much of the parochial school's advantage to the functional community inherent among its constituents. The fact that Catholic schools exhibit good results with non-Catholic children in inner cities shows that community can be created by the school and is not necessarily an extension of pre-existing community within a parish. Coleman found that parochial schools engender a sense of belonging, in part because parents make the conscious choice to send their children to them, thus electing to belong to them. He also pointed to another distinguishing characteristic of parochial schools: a religion-based, foundational assumption that each child, created in the image of God, possesses an individual dignity and worth. That respect for individual worth compels the adults in a child's life, including teachers and other school personnel, to attend to the child's learning and moral development with exceptional devotion and sense of service. Parochial schools also understand the importance of the family to the child's academic success and the value of connection among the families of children who spend their daily lives together in a school. In Coleman's view, intergenerational closure—the connections of communication and association between the child, the child's schoolmates, and the parents of these children—contributes to the social capita available to children and the level of community among the constituents of a school.

What Coleman found in parochial schools exists also in some public schools: a sense of belonging, communication and association among constituents, and devotion to each child's learning and development. Learning standards give schools a value-orientation, a common purpose around which students, teachers, and parents can rally, and a gauge by which each child's progress can be measured as well as the progress of the school as a whole. Some public schools have also been successful in fully engaging parents in the learning lives of their children, promoting a partnership between the family and the school that fosters community and, in turn, a community that fosters partnership.

The connections among the people associated with a school, the intergenerational and intragenerational bonds, the commitment to purpose, and the devotion to each child's success do not occur by happenstance, but by design and careful attention. The Mega System does not give these intangibles short shrift, but provides vehicles through which they can be achieved. The connection between the school and the home, best viewed as the relationships between partners within one community of the school, is paramount. No less important are the connections within each of these groups—parents connected with other parents, teachers with other teachers, and students with other students. The Mega System's concept of shared leadership through teams playing essential roles in decision-making is one of these vehicles. An individualized approach to instruction of a common curriculum is another. Above all, the Mega System promotes a value-based purpose for the school, definition of roles, and clear expectations of the constituents of a school community—students, parents, teachers, school staff, and volunteers. The nexus of expectation and obligation is primal, and upon it trust is built.

> The connections among the people associated with a school, the intergenerational and intragenerational bonds, the commitment to purpose, and the devotion to each child's success do not occur by happenstance, but by design and careful attention.

While this chapter will deal primarily with school-home relationships that encourage parental support for children's learning, the other connections within the school community are no less important. The classroom culture discussed in Chapter 3 emphasizes the essential interactions and relationships between the teacher and students in a classroom that solidify each student's sense of belonging. A student, first and foremost, must feel that the teacher knows him, cares about him, and is vitally concerned about his well-being and progress. That sense of connectedness makes effective instruction possible. Each teacher's sense of connectedness, personal investment in the success of school, and interest in the professional satisfaction of colleagues buoys spirits and makes difficult work rewarding.

The Curriculum of the Home

In Chapter 3, we discussed the school's curriculum—the body of knowledge and set of skills that the school intends for its students to master. The home also has a curriculum. The "curriculum of the home" is the bundle of attitudes, habits, knowledge, and skills that children acquire, through their relationship with their family, that facilitates their school learning. Learning can be propelled, to a certain degree, by a child's innate curiosity and desire for competence, but school learning requires the discipline and persistence to complete assignments and master difficult material long after the initial curiosity has been satisfied. Ideally, parents fan the flames of the child's curiosity and also mold the practical habits and turn of mind that keep the child doggedly on task until the job is done.

The school is most effective when the home does its part. Therefore, the *connection* between the school and the home is essential to school improvement and school success.

The school is most effective when the home does its part. Therefore, the *connection* between the school and the home is essential to school improvement and school success. Helping parents fully engage in the learning lives of their children is a necessary function of the school, and one that requires considerable, consistent, and competent attention. A fruitful connection between the school and the home is built upon purpose, communication, education, and association. Cumulatively, the connections among the teachers, staff, and students form the web of community, a community of the school. A school community is not the school's affiliation with external agencies, nor is it a place. A school community is found in the relationships among the people intimately attached to a school—the students, their teachers, the families of the students, the school's staff, and active volunteers. The people know their school community's *purpose,* what they value in the education of their children, and everyone's role in getting the job done. The members of a school community *communicate* about these values, the expectations they have of one another, the roles they play, and the progress they are making. The members of a school community *educate* themselves and one another to perform their roles more competently. They *associate* with one another to strengthen their relationships and amplify the effects of their individual contributions to children's learning and personal development.

Engaging parents in the learning lives of their children *sounds* like a good idea. In fact, most parents have been engaged in every aspect of their children's lives since their children were born. For a school to guide and channel that natural engagement toward activities that most directly support the child's school learning is an efficient way to improve student learning outcomes. So why is "parent involvement" considered a peripheral aspect of schooling in the frenzied pursuit for gains in assessments in reading, mathematics, science, and social studies? While home environments correlate strongly with student learning outcomes, schools can be dissuaded from investing in their connections with families through a short-sighted focus on what the school does within its walls, during its scheduled day, within the confines of its own methods and its own curriculum. And yet, asked what obstacles they face in achieving the results they desire for their students, teachers will invariably cite inadequacies in parents' preparation of their children for school learning.

The school's success, as measured by the demonstrated accretion of student learning such as we see on achievement tests and standards-based assessments, is the aggregate of the learning of each individual student. In the classroom, we establish a culture that is conducive to learning, and we also target instruction to meet the needs of each student. This same combination of conducive culture and individual attention pertains to the school community and the curriculum of the home. The school community provides the culture that encourages each family to provide the curriculum of the home. Knowing what is included in the curriculum of the home is as important as knowing what is included in the school's curriculum. Just what attitudes, habits, skills, and knowledge do we expect families to instill in children? How does the school community— through purpose, communication, education, and association—build a culture of expectation and support and also provide opportunities for parents to gain greater competence in helping their children master the curriculum of the home?

We use the term "school community" to describe the connections among people intimately attached to a school—students, teachers, staff, parents, volunteers. "Community" is an amorphous term, subject to misuse. It is important to be exact in our use of the term here. We are not speaking of a community as something apart from the school, as in school-community relations. Our reference is to the internal community that binds its members to the school and to each other. We speak of a face-to-face community among the people who share a common devotion to the children in their midst, including

Knowing what is included in the curriculum of the home is as important as knowing what is included in the school's curriculum.

Home

School

The Curriculum of the Home

the children themselves. This community is strengthened when it is made distinct, when its values, rituals, traditions, and practices are distinctly its own. It is a true community when its members are in association with one another, communicating with one another about the values they share, the progress they make, and the roles each of its members plays.

Figure 1 shows the interactions among school and home variables that impact school learning and student success, within a community of the two. While this schematic focuses on the school community and its impact on family behaviors, a similar graphic might demonstrate the school community's effects on the teachers and other school personnel. The box in the figure called "school community" represents the relationships among the people intimately attached to the school. In reality, these relationships are not something apart from "schooling," but are an aspect of schooling that deserves special notice. Just as the school's programs, schedules, curriculum, decision-making structures, and instructional methods are developed intentionally, so must the relationships among the members of the school community be fostered by design, understood, tended to, measured, and brought to a standard of excellence.

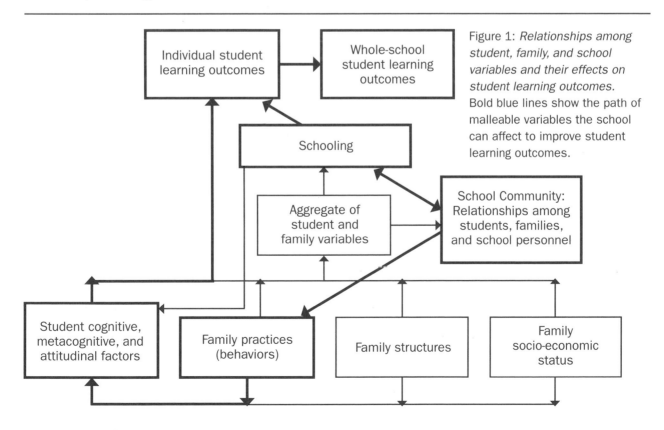

Figure 1: *Relationships among student, family, and school variables and their effects on student learning outcomes.* Bold blue lines show the path of malleable variables the school can affect to improve student learning outcomes.

IMPORTANT RULE

Within the school community, the important rule is to not let family structure and family socioeconomic status become conversation stoppers.

Figure 1 differentiates among family structures, family socioeconomic status, and family practices. Family structure includes the number of parents and other adults in the home and the number and ages of the children. Family socioeconomic status includes the family financial circumstances and parents' level of education. Family practices include the routines of family life, the relationships among its members, and the actual behaviors of family members. The curriculum of the home resides in family practices, although it would be unrealistic to underestimate the mitigating influences of family size and family financial resources on family practices. Within the school community, the important rule is to not let family structure and family socioeconomic status become conversation stoppers. Instead, the conversation must revolve around family practices, with creativity and insight applied in helping parents overcome the weight of difficult circumstances in order to maintain the relationships with their children that encourage constructive attitudes, habits, and skills. The family's poverty does not negate the child's need for nurture or the school's obligation to help parents understand their role. The absence of a father in the home makes the job tougher for mom, but the child's needs remain the same nonetheless. Recognizing this fact, the school can help mom get the job done.

While the curriculum of the home provides a behavioral checklist of family practices that predict children's school success, we are discovering that much must be read between the lines. Somewhere in the parent-child relationship, children acquire a sense of expectation and perception of their own efficacy in "measuring up." Children internalize their parents' expectations of them regarding school learning, and they also absorb signals from parents as to their own ability to meet these expectations. William Jeynes (2002) found the nuances of parent-child communication regarding expectations to be a particularly powerful source of motivation for minority children and children living in poverty. These children especially benefit from visions of what is possible for them beyond the circumstances in which they find themselves at the time, and their parents contribute both to that vision and to the children's confidence that they can reach out and attain it (Hoover-Dempsey, 2005).

Henderson and Mapp (2002) conducted a thorough review of two decades of research on parent involvement, structuring their examination around three topics: studies on the impact of family and community involvement on student achievement; studies on effective strategies to connect schools, families, and community;

The Curriculum of the Home

and studies on parent and community organizing efforts to improve schools. There is substantial evidence that family engagement in children's learning is beneficial, but the evidence that school-based initiatives can influence family behaviors in ways that impact learning is limited to small-scale investigations of specific strategies that are productive for those families that most directly access them. Studies of whole-school effects are typically *ex post facto*, in the tradition of effective schools research that examines the characteristics of successful schools rather than validating the value added to learning by experimental interventions.

Not letting family circumstances stop the ongoing conversation between the school and parents depends upon respect for the potential of every family to do better by its children.

From the evidence available, Henderson and Mapp draw convincing conclusions about the characteristics of successful school efforts to engage families. Most specifically, effective school initiatives to engage parents: 1) build a foundation of trust and respect, 2) connect parent-engagement strategies to learning objectives, and 3) reach out to engage parents beyond the school. These three qualities are found in schools where parent involvement is measurably high, in specific programs that demonstrate effects on learning outcomes, and in schools that exhibit high levels of achievement. Henderson and Mapp echo the conclusions of Swap (1993) that effective parent engagement must be comprehensive in nature, with the school consistently interfacing with parents at many points, in many venues, over the course of the schooling years.

Not letting family circumstances stop the ongoing conversation between the school and parents depends upon respect for the potential of every family to do better by its children. Patricia Edwards (2004) writes persuasively of *differentiated parenting*, admonishing us not to place all parents into one basket. When we design programs for parents, one size will not fit all. Edwards uses the term *parentally appropriate* to stress the point that "because parents are different, tasks and activities must be compatible with their capabilities" (p. 83). This is not to say that parents' goals for their children vary (they all want their children to succeed in school); their situations, perspectives, and abilities affect their capacity to support their children in particular ways. For example, asking parents to read to their children appears to be a simple request. But some parents have not received, as children themselves, the modeling of how to read interactively with children. Neither might they know just what materials are most appropriate for children to read at any point in time. They also may underestimate the positive effects of talking with their children about what the children have read. These parents, then, require different support than parents who might readily respond to the request to "read to your child" because of their own past experience.

The point Edwards makes is more subtle and significant than merely matching the school's request of parents with each parent's ability to respond. The greater point is that parents, like students, are best served when treated individually. This means knowing them, listening to their own stories, understanding what will be most helpful to them in raising their children and supporting their children's school learning. A parent's needs are not static; they change over time with the advancing age of their children. Parent programs require a scope and sequence, differentiation to meet the needs of the parent relative to the age and progress of the child.

Trust and mutual respect cut in both directions; school personnel must operate from a basis of trust in parents, and parents must trust the school. The relationship is circular, of course, since people trust those who trust them and respect those who show them respect. The beginning point lies with the school staff, since it is more manageable to first assure that the limited number of school personnel approach families with a constructive frame of mind than to attempt to change the hearts and minds of all the parents. Does the school countenance idle chatter, often driven by frustration, about parents who "don't care"? Does the principal help teachers look beyond the obstacles of family circumstance to find solutions for children that include clear expectations of, and support for, their parents? Overgeneralization from worst cases can become epidemic in a school, attributing to many families the deficiencies seen in a few families. "You don't understand," the frustrated teacher might say, "we have kids whose parents are on drugs and who let their kids run wild." Yes, every school has its small core of families in which children are drastically short-changed. But that doesn't stop the conversation. What about the other families? And what can we do for that small group of families that are, to use the term arbitrarily applied to them, "dysfunctional"?

The answer is two-fold: We never stop expecting all parents to give their children what they need from home in order to succeed in school, and we find the best possible compensatory measures for the recalcitrant few. The best possible compensatory measures most often include time and attention for these children from caring adults other than their parents—community volunteers in the school, after-

Trust and mutual respect cut in both directions; school personnel must operate from a basis of trust in parents, and parents must trust the school. The relationship is circular, of course, since people trust those who trust them and respect those who show them respect.

The Curriculum of the Home

school programs, and participation in youth activities provided by solid organizations such as Boys & Girls Clubs, 4-H, YMCAs, YWCAs, Boy Scouts, and Girl Scouts. Providing these best possible compensatory measures doesn't happen willy-nilly, but by careful matching of each child with the right resource.

While overgeneralization from the worst cases of family dysfunction is one roadblock a school can throw in its own path toward effective connection with families, some schools operate within attendance areas where the prevailing culture insufficiently encourages children's academic success. When a child grows up amidst indolence, violence, immediate gratification, and low regard for civilizing institutions such as the school, the effects are monstrously adverse. When most of the children attending a school come from a neighborhood steeped in a culture of dissipation and failure, the effects on the school are profoundly burdensome. In such situations, the school must provide a cultural counterweight for children and not reflect or permit the self-destructive behaviors that may prevail outside its doors. Typically, the school is the island of hope in these seas of despair. The school is also a source of positive influence on the culture that surrounds it, and its positive influences are extended family by family for the sake of each child. Even here, each parent deserves the expectation that he or she will rise to the task, and the task must be made clear. The task for the parent is to provide the child with a curriculum of the home. Again, while consistently expecting the best of each parent and supporting their efforts, the school simultaneously seeks compensatory experiences for the child. No compensatory experience is more important than a relationship with a caring adult who shows the child the route to success, the way out of the culture of despair and irresponsibility. Resilient children defy the negative outcomes their circumstances predict. Resilient families stand apart from the destructive pressures of the culture that surrounds them. Resilient neighborhoods reverse the habits of failure that previously defined them. The school has a missionary capacity to produce resilient children, resilient families, and resilient neighborhoods.

Expectations and behaviors are the cultural and familial presses that bear upon children. Expectations and behaviors are inextricably webbed; parents express their expectations for their children not only in their words but in their actions. Schools express their expectations for their students and their students' parents through what they profess and in the way they operate.

What, then, do we expect of all parents so that each child receives the support from home necessary to success in school? We expect parents to provide the curriculum of the home, and we must be clear about our expectations, revisiting them often, communicating about them, educating parents about them, and centering our associations upon them. The curriculum of the home is as specific and tangible as the curriculum of the school, based on its own standards. Research on the curriculum of the home (e.g., Bloom, 1964, 1981; Marjoribanks, 1979; Walberg, 1984) provides a description of family practices that link to school performance. Those family practices include aspects of the parent-child relationship, the routines of family life, and family expectations and supervision.

The Parent-Child Relationship

A parent-child relationship most conducive to children's school learning is based on a bond of love, demonstrated through expressions of affection that give the child a sense of worth, security, and support. The verbal exchanges between parent and child contribute to the child's developing facility with language, vocabulary, and interest in words and ideas. When parents converse with their children about daily events, in personal and sustained conversation, the child grows in his or her ability to analyze, to express, and to listen. The child's interest in the broader world is stimulated, and the parent maintains a close awareness of what is going on in the child's life—at school, with friends, and in the child's interpretation of his place in the world. When parents encourage children to use new words and to enjoy the play of words, they keep alive the child's natural inclination to expand her vocabulary and gain power through verbal expression. Family discussion of books, newspapers, magazines, television programs, and other language-laden media also encourage both language development and richer associations with a multitude of topics. Finally, families that make visits to libraries, museums, zoos, historical sites, and cultural events demonstrate the value and excitement of learning to their children and associate this learning with family togetherness.

The Curriculum of the Home

The Routine of Family Life

Children thrive when their parents provide them with the security and discipline of a daily routine, the boundaries of expected times for eating, sleeping, playing, working, studying, and reading. Family activities centered around hobbies, games, and other activities that require collective engagement, thinking, and verbal exchange bolster children's ability to concentrate, to explore, to find pleasure in mutual endeavor. School-age children need a quiet place to study and read and the discipline to place a priority on these activities. A formal study time in the home, regardless of the assignments sent home by teachers, not only forms the habit of daily study, but also establishes learning as a family value.

Family Expectations and Supervision

From the example and expectations of their parents, children learn to do their best whatever the task, to honor the importance of punctuality, and to give schoolwork priority over other activities. The parents' encouragement to use correct, effective, and appropriate language forms a child's readiness for the language-rich environment of the school. When parents monitor their children's use of time, the quality of their televiewing, their use of computer games and the internet, and their associations with peers, children learn to place proper value on competing interests. Parental knowledge of their children's progress in school and their personal growth, gained in part from close communication with teachers, helps emphasize the importance of learning and provides parents with the information necessary to make the best decisions about their children's schooling.

These descriptions of family life may sound idealistic, like cliché vignettes of the perfect family. In fact, they are. They also describe the home environments that all children find beneficial to their school success, and therefore, they are worth pursuing. Only with an eye to the ideal can we guide parents toward improved support for their children's learning, a goal that all parents share. The components of the curriculum of the home are within the reach of nearly every family, although some families' situations require more discipline and effort from them than do others. In a single-parent home, the children's needs remain the same, but one parent must assume the responsibilities otherwise shared by two. In a large family, each child needs all that the curriculum of the home entails, but the parents

> Parental knowledge of their children's progress in school and their personal growth, gained in part from close communication with teachers, helps emphasize the importance of learning and provides parents with the information necessary to make the best decisions about their children's schooling.

The Curriculum of the Home

must spread their attention across a nest full of hungry beaks. In the clutch of poverty, parents must be assured that what their children need most they are still able to provide. When the language of school is not the language of home, parents may still affirm that words matter, stories convey meaning, and books open doors to all worlds.

The school cannot substitute for the powerful potentiality of the family; it can only encourage the family to apply its advantages to the benefit of the child.

In listing the components of the curriculum of the home, the behavioral correlates with school learning, it is easy to miss the underlying potency of what a family provides that cannot be found elsewhere. Habits and values are formed in the home because they are attached to the fibers of loving relationships; the bonds of attachment make the particulars of behavior fecund. The school cannot substitute for the powerful potentiality of the family; it can only encourage the family to apply its advantages to the benefit of the child.

Effective Parent/ Family Programs

An effective parent/family program is one that helps parents provide the curriculum of the home. Henderson and Berla (1994) advise that successful parent programs must be: 1) **comprehensive** (reaching all families, not just those most easily engaged, and involving parents in a variety of roles), 2) **well-planned** (with specific goals and clear communication of what is expected of all parties), and 3) **long-lasting** (as opposed to the typical, short-term project). Epstein's (1995) typology of family involvement in children's education has become the standard of the field and appears in various adaptations, including the National Standards for Parent Involvement set forth by the PTA. A comprehensive family-school partnership (which Epstein defines as an ongoing relationship rather than a program or event) would address all six types of family involvement. Epstein's six types of parent engagement are:

- **Parenting** (helping families provide their children the necessary care, safety, affection, discipline, and guidance)
- **Communicating** (maintaining a variety of effective, two-way communications between school and home about the school programs, the school's expectations of parents, and children's progress)
- **Volunteering** (providing and encouraging opportunities for parents to help out at school and with school activities)
- **Learning at Home** (providing information and support for parents to monitor homework, provide family learning activities, and encourage reading habits at home)
- **Decision Making** (including parents in school decisions, especially those that most directly affect families, and developing parent leaders and representatives)
- **Collaborating with the Community** (bringing community resources to the service of the school)

Early childhood programs that teach parents to work with their children at home have proven effective in preparing the children for school (Baker, Piotrkowski, & Brooks-Gunn, 1998; Mathematica, 2001; Starkey & Klein, 2000). For school-age children, comprehensive efforts to engage parents at

> An effective parent/family program is one that helps parents provide the curriculum of the home. Successful parent programs must be:
>
> 1) comprehensive
> 2) well-planned
> 3) long-lasting

Effective Parent/Family Programs

various points and in different ways seem most productive (Gordon, 1979; Swap, 1993). A 2002 study by Westat and Policy Studies Associates for the U.S. Department of Education considered student achievement in 71 Title I elementary schools. The study looked at the connection between the school's practices of outreach to parents and improvement in reading and math by low-performing students. The relationship between outreach to parents and student learning gains was the strongest of all the variables considered in the study. Outreach was measured along three scales:

- Meeting face-to-face;
- Sending materials on ways to help their child at home; and
- Telephoning both routinely and when their child was having problems.

The three points distilled from Henderson and Mapp (2002) provide the most concise set of linchpins to successful school-home relationships:

- Build a foundation of trust and respect;
- Make direct connections to children's learning; and
- Reach out to parents in their homes and communities.

Elaborating on these points provides the fundamentals of program design for effective, school-based, family and parent initiatives. It is also important to reiterate that the reason schools should take steps to engage parents is so the school's own effectiveness is improved; children learn best when they benefit from good teaching *and* a supportive home environment. It behooves schools to:

- **Provide parents with clear, consistent expectations**, information and guidance to help them practice specific family behaviors (the curriculum of the home) that enhance children's school learning;
- **Maintain convenient channels of two-way communication** between parents and teachers;
- **Bring parents together** on occasion to encourage their sharing of norms, standards, and child-rearing experiences;
- **Provide parents with educational programs** to build their capacity to maintain a strong curriculum of the home; and
- **Provide teachers with professional development** and consistent policies to build their capacity to work with parents and to reinforce the school's clear expectations of parents.

Purpose

Borrowing from business management concepts for defining, articulating, and focusing an organization's activities on its essential purpose, schools have commonly created statements of vision, mission, and purpose. That is a useful exercise, but too often the statements are generic and insufficiently attached to practices. The Mega System, through the decision-making structures described in Chapter 2, provides avenues to align practices with purpose. Extending the definition of school community to include the families of students, we need particular links between purpose and practice to assist the school community in engaging parents and making them full partners.

The School Community Council (SCC) provides a venue for shared leadership and articulation of policies and practices relative to families consistent with the school community's purpose.

The School Community Council is the structure suggested within the Mega System to give focused attention to the area of overlapping responsibility between the home and the school within a community of the two. The School Community Council (SCC) provides a venue for shared leadership and articulation of policies and practices relative to families consistent with the school community's purpose. Especially, the SCC attends to the areas in which the school and home most commonly interface. The SCC also assists parents in understanding and providing the curriculum of the home, and it provides ways to supplement the curriculum of the home for children whose parents do not provide the parent-child relationships, routine of family life, and supervision and expectation that all children need.

To make the SCC an effective body, it needs its own constitution, by-laws, and official status within the school's system of governance. To be productive, the SCC also needs a scope of work and specific duties to perform. Additionally, its members must be trained in the research and best practices of parenting, parent programs, and team functioning. Above all, the SCC must be respected through the active participation of the principal and the serious application of its directives.

The SCC is ideally suited to outline the roles of parents, teachers, and students in a School Community Compact, a document commonly found in schools and often inadequately applied. The Compact is useful when it is the subject of discussion among students, teachers, and parents, and when they are challenged to meet its expectations. Similarly, learning standards offer concrete support for the school's purpose and guide instruction. Helping parents understand learning

Purpose

standards and see their role in supporting their children's mastery of standards is a job the SCC assumes effectively within its scope of work. Likewise, the school's improvement plan is an evolving document that merits wide understanding within the school community. Homework, often the primary interface between school learning and home activity, requires school-wide policies understood by parents as well as teachers and students, with the role of each clearly defined.

Whenever parents meet with school personnel, the school's purpose and its supporting documents can be discussed and reinforced. The supporting documents include the Compact, learning standards, improvement plan, and homework policy. An ongoing conversation between parents and teachers around these documents builds understanding and a sense of common endeavor toward each student's success. The open house and parent-teacher-student conference are typical points of contact between parents and school personnel, and each can be planned to advance an understanding of the school community's purpose, each member's role in that purpose, and the relevance to each child.

Communication

"What we have here is a failure to communicate," said the prison guard in the movie *Cool Hand Luke*. How often do we say the same in schools? Clear communication requires more than the opportunity to communicate, it also requires an agreement on the topics for discussion. Communication between the school and the home includes five essential topics: 1) what parents can expect from the school—its programs, curriculum, activities, procedures, and policies; 2) what the school can expect from parents—the curriculum of the home; 3) how the parents' child is progressing; 4) how the school can help the parents; and 5) how the parents can help the school. Typically, schools are good at providing information about their programs and some indication of how the child is progressing. The school probably provides some avenues for two-way communication about these two topics. A greater challenge lies in giving due attention to what the school should expect from parents, how the school can help parents in their role, and how parents can help the school in its role. Also, most schools need to work hard at creating opportunities for true communication, conversation, between parents and school personnel, and between parents and other parents. This requires outreach to parents, and it requires careful linkage between parent-child interactions and school learning.

Because opportunity for communication between the home and the school is limited if it only occurs when parents are at the school, the school must find avenues for outreach to the home. Two forms of outreach are especially beneficial: instructional links and home visits. Instructional links are assignments to students that serve three purposes: require parent-child interaction, link to school learning, and educate parents about school learning. They are a special kind of homework. Reading School-Home Links, available from the U. S. Department of Education, provide interactive reading activities aligned to standards from kindergarten through third grade. Similar links are available in other subject areas and other grade levels. School policies and professional development for teachers can encourage teachers to develop their own school-home links, serving the three purposes of 1) interactivity between parent and child, 2) connection to school learning, and 3) education of parents about school learning.

FORMS OF OUTREACH

Because opportunity for communication between the home and the school is limited if it only occurs when parents are at the school, the school must find avenues for outreach to the home. Two forms of outreach are especially beneficial: instructional links and home visits.

Communication

Home visits and home gather-ings are forms of outreach that facilitate two-way commu-nication and circumvent the complaint that some parents don't come to the school.

Home visits and home gatherings are forms of outreach that facilitate two-way communication and circumvent the complaint that some parents don't come to the school. A home visit is when someone representing the school visits a student's home. A home gathering is when parents gather in one parent's home and someone representing the school is included. Home visits may be conducted by teachers or by others—parents, community members, teacher aides—trained for the job. At a home gathering, a teacher is the most effective "official" participant from the school.

For both home visits and home gatherings, good organization is the key. Home visitors are trained and given a purpose for the visit. For example, the homes of primary grade students might be visited in the early summer to talk with parents about the importance of children's reading at home and maybe to give them books for the children to read. Visits might focus on parents of students entering a new school, such as kindergarteners or students entering the first grade of a middle school or high school. The visitor would provide parents with a welcome to the school and orientation materials. Whatever the specific purpose of the visit, the occasion is perfect for giving parents helpful information about the school, particularly to inform them of programs for parents. A packet with a welcoming letter from the principal is a nice touch. The visit is conversational, with a "get-to-know-you" feel.

Home gatherings require their own preparation and training for the host parents and the participating teachers. They meet as a group to develop an agenda for the gatherings and to plan the logistics. Each host parent develops a list of invitees. Teachers may suggest to the group parents who would especially benefit from a home gathering, but each host parent must be allowed to select his or her own invitee list. Ground rules are important. The gathering is not a time to discuss particular children or teachers, and the host parent and visiting teacher need to know how to divert conversations that drift in that direction. The home gathering is a good time to talk about the roles of parents and of teachers, in general, in supporting the purpose of the school. The discussion is led by the host parent. The mood is informal, with a handful of parents, a pot of coffee, a few cookies, and an agenda that guides their conversation. Once a round of home gatherings has taken place, the host parents and teachers meet again to discuss their experience.

Education

The school community is a learning community, and teachers and parents are learners as well as the students. The SCC can plan educational opportunities for teachers to build their skills in working with parents. The SCC can plan parent education programs. Some parent education programs may take the form of the typical "event," with a speaker or group sessions led by other parents or teachers. An especially productive, high-quality parent education program might span two or three meetings of a small group of parents, led by a parent, with a curriculum to study and discuss. Multiple sessions allow the group to jell and parents to get to know each other. Topics for these sessions might be drawn from the curriculum of the home—supporting children's reading habits and study habits at home; encouraging respectful and responsible behavior; or getting pre-schoolers ready for school. A parent course for parents of children with disabilities might help parents support the learning of children with special needs, provide an opportunity for parents to share experiences, and increase parents' understanding of special education. The curriculum contains informational content, opportunities for discussion, and activities to carry out with children between sessions.

Association

Association means face-to-face connection among members of the school community. An association provides a venue for parents to get to know other parents, parents and teachers to get to know each other better, and an opportunity for everyone to strengthen their understanding of the school community's purpose and their role relative to it. Some associations include students. Within a school community, an association is a way to bridge divisions among students; older students reading with younger students, for example. An association may bring volunteer parents and community members to the school to work with individual students or small groups of students. An association may be a common experience, an event shared by all students, possibly one including parents such as a Family Night. Family Reading Nights are a typical common experience that gathers students, parents, and teachers for an evening focused on reading. Similar events can be planned for other subject and interest areas, filled with interactive, parent-child activities. In essence, an association brings together members of the school community to focus on a topic consistent with the school's purpose.

Chapter Summary

This chapter has outlined ways to connect members of the school community to one another to promote the purposes of the school community. The School Community Council is a vehicle for giving special attention to these connections, planning them and providing them. The School Community Council is an official component in the school's governance structure, with its own constitution and by-laws to define its purpose and means of operation. The School Community Council consists of the principal, parents, and key personnel, such as a teacher representative, counselor, and parent liaison. The majority of members should be parents. This chapter also reviewed the curriculum of the home, the important parent-child interactions and family routines that support school learning. Key documents that express the purpose of the school—Compact, school improvement plan, learning standards, and homework policy—are central to the ongoing conversation between parents and other parents, and between parents and school personnel. These conversations build a sense of community around the purposes of the school. The SCC provides one means of shared leadership in the school community, and communication, education, and association are categories of connection around which the SCC's activities may be organized.

Putting Connection Components in Place

The forms on the following page may be used to assess the current status of key elements of connection and to plan for the development of the missing pieces. A Leadership Team can work through these forms, develop a plan of action, and monitor the progress. For items checked "No" on the assessment of the current situation, primary responsibility is assigned to a person or team, with an expected date for completion of the task.

Connection Indicators

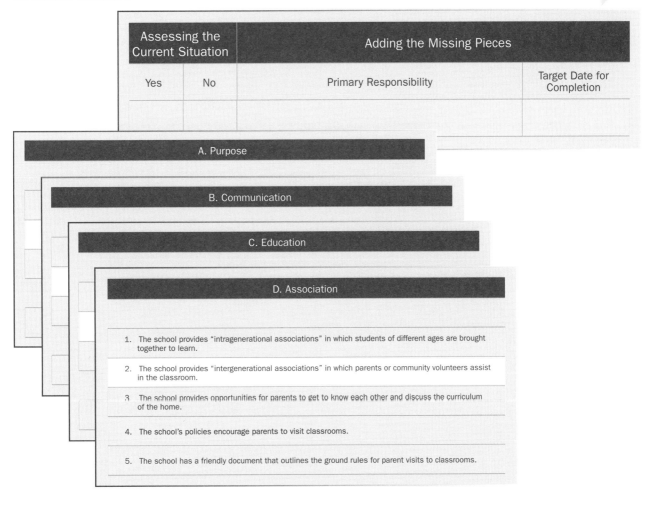

Assessing the Current Situation		Adding the Missing Pieces	
Yes	No	Primary Responsibility	Target Date for Completion

A. Purpose

B. Communication

C. Education

D. Association

1. The school provides "intragenerational associations" in which students of different ages are brought together to learn.

2. The school provides "intergenerational associations" in which parents or community volunteers assist in the classroom.

3. The school provides opportunities for parents to get to know each other and discuss the curriculum of the home.

4. The school's policies encourage parents to visit classrooms.

5. The school has a friendly document that outlines the ground rules for parent visits to classrooms.

Connection Indicators

A. Purpose	
1. The school's mission statement is distinct, clear, and focused on student learning.	
2. The school's Compact outlines the responsibilities/expectations of teachers, parents, and students.	
3. The school's Compact includes responsibilities/expectations of parents drawn from the curriculum of the home.	
4. The school's Compact is annually distributed to teachers, school personnel, parents, and students.	
5. The school's homework policy provides guidelines for amount of daily study time at home by grade level.	
6. The school's homework policy requires homework at all grade levels.	
7. The school's homework policy makes homework a part of the student's report card grade.	
8. The school's homework policy stresses the importance of checking, marking, and promptly returning homework.	
9. The school's mission statement, Compact, and homework policy are included in the school improvement plan.	
10. The school celebrates its accomplishments.	
11. The school recognizes the individual accomplishments of teachers.	
12. The school recognizes the accomplishments of teams.	

| Assessing the Current Situation | | Adding the Missing Pieces | |
Yes	No	Primary Responsibility	Target Date for Completion

Connection Indicators

B. Communication	
1. The school's Compact, homework policy, and learning standards are routinely reviewed and discussed at faculty meetings.	
2. The school's Compact, homework policy, and learning standards are routinely reviewed and discussed at open houses and parent-teacher conferences.	
3. Parent-teacher conferences are held at least twice a year and include students at least once a year.	
4. The school regularly and clearly communicates with parents about its expectations of them and the importance of the curriculum of the home.	
5. The "ongoing conversation" between school personnel and teachers is candid, supportive, and flows in both directions.	
6. The school maintains a program of home visits by teachers, staff, and/or trained community members.	
7. Teachers regularly make "interactive" assignments that encourage parent-child interaction relative to school learning.	
8. The school maintains a program of home gatherings, with groups of parents meeting in a home with a teacher.	
9. Teachers are familiar with the curriculum of the home and discuss it with parents.	
10. Parents are familiar with the curriculum of the home and discuss it with teachers.	

Assessing the Current Situation		Adding the Missing Pieces	
Yes	No	Primary Responsibility	Target Date for Completion

Connection Indicators

C. Education

1. The school offers parent education programs focused on building skills relative to the curriculum of the home.

2. Parent education programs are led by trained parent leaders.

3. Parent education programs include some multi-session group experiences with specific agendas or curricula.

4. Professional development programs for teachers include assistance in working effectively with parents.

D. Association

1. The school provides "intragenerational associations" in which students of different ages are brought together to learn.

2. The school provides "intergenerational associations" in which parents or community volunteers assist in the classroom.

3. The school provides opportunities for parents to get to know each other and discuss the curriculum of the home.

4. The school's policies encourage parents to visit classrooms.

5. The school has a friendly document that outlines the ground rules for parent visits to classrooms.

6. The school sponsors all-school events that include parents, students, and teachers and focus on aspects of student learning.

7. All-school events include parent-child interactive activities.

8. Office and support staff are trained to make the school a "welcoming place" for parents.

Assessing the Current Situation		Adding the Missing Pieces		
Yes	No	Primary Responsibility		Target Date for Completion

Assessing the Current Situation		Adding the Missing Pieces		
Yes	No	Primary Responsibility		Target Date for Completion

Chapter 4 References

Baker, A. J. L., Piotrkowski, C. S., & Brooks-Gunn, J. (1998). The effects of the Home Instruction Program for Preschool Youngsters (HIPPY) on children's school performance at the end of the program and one year later. *Early Childhood Research Quarterly, 13*(4), 571-588.

Bloom, B. S. (1964). *Stability and change in human characteristics.* New York: Wiley.

Bloom, B. S. (1981). *All our children learning: A primer for parents, teachers, and other educators.* New York: McGraw-Hill.

Coleman, J. S. (1987, August-September). Families and schools. *Educational Researcher,* 36-37.

Coleman, J. S. (1990). *Foundations of social theory.* Cambridge, MA: Harvard University Press.

Coleman, J. S., & Hoffer, T. (1987). *Public and private high schools: The impact of communities.* New York: Basic Books.

Edwards, P. (2004). *Children's literacy development.* Boston: Pearson Education, Inc.

Epstein, J. L. (1995). School/family/community partnerships: Caring for the children we share. *Phi Delta Kappan, 76*(9), 701-712.

Gordon, I. J. (1979, July). How has Follow Through promoted parent involvement? *Young Children, 34*(5), 49-53.

Jeynes, W. H. (2002). A meta-analysis. The effects of parental involvement on minority children's academic achievement. *Education and Urban Society, 35*(2), 202-219.

Henderson, A. T., & Berla, N. (1994). *The family is critical to student achievement.* Washington, DC: National Center for Law and Education.

Henderson, A., & Mapp. K. (2002). *A new wave of evidence: The impact of school, family, and community connections on student achievement.* Austin, TX: Southwest Educational Development Laboratory.

Hoover-Dempsey, K. V. (2005). *The social context of parental involvement: A path to enhanced achievement.* Report to the Institute of Educational Sciences, U. S. Department of Education. Retrieved May 14, 2005 from http://www.vanderbilt.edu/Peabody/family-school/Reports.html.

Marjoribanks, K. (1979). *Ethnic families and children's achievement.* Sydney: George Allen & Unwin.

Mathematica Policy Research, Inc., & Center for Children and Families at Teachers College, Columbia University. (2001). *Building their futures: How early Head Start programs are enhancing the lives of infants and toddlers in low-income families.* Princeton, NJ: Mathematica Policy Research, Inc.

Sergiovanni, T. (1999). *Building community in schools.* San Francisco: Jossey-Bass.

Starkey, P., & Klein, A. (2000). Fostering parental support for children's mathematical development: An intervention with Head Start families. *Early Education and Development, 11*(5), 659-680.

Swap, S. (1993). *Developing home-school partnerships: From concepts to practice.* New York: Teachers' College Press, Columbia University.

Walberg, H. J. (1984). Families as partners in educational productivity. *Phi Delta Kappan, 65*, 397-400.

Westat and Policy Studies Associates. (2002). *The longitudinal evaluation of school change and performance in Title I schools: Vol. 1. Executive Summary.* Washington, DC: U.S. Department of Education.